Dr. Jeeva Jose
Dr. P. Sojan Lal

Gaining Insight into User and Search Engine Behaviour by Analyzing Web Logs

Anchor Academic
Publishing

Jose, Jeeva, Lal, P. Sojan: Gaining Insight into User and Search Engine Behaviour by Analyzing Web Logs, Hamburg, Anchor Academic Publishing 2016

Buch-ISBN: 978-3-96067-087-2
PDF-eBook-ISBN: 978-3-96067-587-7
Druck/Herstellung: Anchor Academic Publishing, Hamburg, 2016

Bibliografische Information der Deutschen Nationalbibliothek:
Die Deutsche Nationalbibliothek verzeichnet diese Publikation in der Deutschen Nationalbibliografie; detaillierte bibliografische Daten sind im Internet über http://dnb.d-nb.de abrufbar.

Bibliographical Information of the German National Library:
The German National Library lists this publication in the German National Bibliography. Detailed bibliographic data can be found at: http://dnb.d-nb.de

All rights reserved. This publication may not be reproduced, stored in a retrieval system or transmitted, in any form or by any means, electronic, mechanical, photocopying, recording or otherwise, without the prior permission of the publishers.

Das Werk einschließlich aller seiner Teile ist urheberrechtlich geschützt. Jede Verwertung außerhalb der Grenzen des Urheberrechtsgesetzes ist ohne Zustimmung des Verlages unzulässig und strafbar. Dies gilt insbesondere für Vervielfältigungen, Übersetzungen, Mikroverfilmungen und die Einspeicherung und Bearbeitung in elektronischen Systemen.

Die Wiedergabe von Gebrauchsnamen, Handelsnamen, Warenbezeichnungen usw. in diesem Werk berechtigt auch ohne besondere Kennzeichnung nicht zu der Annahme, dass solche Namen im Sinne der Warenzeichen- und Markenschutz-Gesetzgebung als frei zu betrachten wären und daher von jedermann benutzt werden dürften.

Die Informationen in diesem Werk wurden mit Sorgfalt erarbeitet. Dennoch können Fehler nicht vollständig ausgeschlossen werden und die Diplomica Verlag GmbH, die Autoren oder Übersetzer übernehmen keine juristische Verantwortung oder irgendeine Haftung für evtl. verbliebene fehlerhafte Angaben und deren Folgen.

Alle Rechte vorbehalten

© Anchor Academic Publishing, Imprint der Diplomica Verlag GmbH
Hermannstal 119k, 22119 Hamburg
http://www.diplomica-verlag.de, Hamburg 2016
Printed in Germany

Abstract

Web Usage Mining also known as Web Log Mining is the result of user interaction with a Web server including Web logs, click streams and database transaction or the visits of search engine crawlers at a Website. Log files provide immense source of information about the behavior of users as well as search engine crawlers. Web Usage Mining concerns usage of common browsing patterns i.e. pages requested in sequence from Web logs. These patterns are often referred to us rules and can be utilized to enhance the design and modification of a Website. Analyzing and discovering user behavior is helpful for understanding what online information users inquire and how they behave. The analyzed result can be used in intelligent online applications, refining Websites, improving search accuracy when seeking information and lead decision makers towards better decisions in changing markets like putting advertisements in ideal places. Similarly the crawlers or spiders are accessing the Websites to index new and updated pages. These traces help to analyze the behavior of search engine crawlers.

The log files are unstructured files and of huge size. These files need to be extracted and pre-processed before any data mining functionality to follow. Pre-processing is done in unique way for each application. Two pre-processing algorithms are proposed based on indiscernibility relations in rough set theory which generates Equivalence Classes. The first algorithm generates a pre-processed file with successful user requests while the second one generates a pre-processed file for pre-fetching and caching purposes. Two algorithms are proposed to extract usage analytics. The first algorithm identifies the origin of visits, the top referring sites and the most popular keywords used by the visitor to arrive at a Website. The second algorithm extracts user agents like browser with its version and operating system with its version used by a visitor to access a Website.

Clustering of users based on *Entry Pages* to a Website is done to analyze the deep linked traffic at a Website. The *Top Ten Entry Pages*, the traffic and the temporal information of the *Top Ten Entry Pages* is also studied. Unlike traditional k-means, the number of clusters need not be given as input. Likewise the similar user sessions based on *Entry Pages* are obtained by clustering the user sessions. A Rank Order Clustering algorithm is used for clustering similar user sessions. Two data sets are used, the former one is of a business organization and the latter one is that of an academic institution. The algorithm is tested on two data sets and the results revealed that the percentage of similar user sessions varies from 18.48% to 40.54% in data set 1 and from 28.57% to 66.67% in data set 2.

The sequence length of visitors entered through Home pages and other pages is analyzed. Similarly the sequence length of single visits and repeated visits is also analyzed. A Two Sample Test is employed for testing the hypothesis and the same is repeated for three months in data set 1 and two months in data set 2 to analyze the temporal behavior. The test results revealed that the sequence length of visitors entered through Home page is more than that of visitors entered through other pages. The results also showed that there is a decrease in sequence length in repeated visits. It is found that there is no change in these results over time. A rough set approach is used to classify content and navigational pages in a Website. The results are useful in target advertising.

An extensive study of the search engine crawlers is done to identify their behavior. The log files of two different organizations are pre-processed and extracted to identify the various search engine crawlers visiting the Website. The crawlers accessing these sites are different in number. It is found that first data set is accessed by more number of crawlers or the visibility is more rather than the second data set. The number of visits and pages crawled is studied for both data sets and Kruskal Wallis H Test on these data sets showed that there is a significant difference between the number of visits and pages crawled by various search engine crawlers. Temporal behavior of crawlers is also studied to analyze the time spent by search engine crawlers at Websites. The time plot of various search engine crawlers revealed that there is a significant difference in the time spent between the crawlers. To study the differences in time delay between visits of search engine crawlers, ANOVA and a subsequent Duncan's Multiple Range Test is done. The mean plot and Duncan's Multiple Range test revealed that the time delay of search engine crawlers including Googlebot, Feedfetcher-Google and Ichiro is almost similar. Similarly the crawlers Slurp, Bingbot and Baiduspider showed a similar time delay which is higher than that of the first set of crawlers including Googlebot. All other crawlers showed significant time delay in visiting the Website. This shows that certain crawlers like Googlebot, Feedfetcher-Google, Ichiro, Slurp, Bingbot and Baiduspider are very dynamic compared to other crawlers like Ezooms, MJ12bot, Sosospider etc. Among the 22 crawlers, Googlebot showed least time delay for repeated visits and exhibited consistency in its behavior.

A forecasting model in time series has been proposed for predicting the number of pages crawled by search engine crawlers. A single exponential smoothing method is used to develop the forecasting model. This model is compared with actual values and it is found feasible. The time delay between two consecutive visits of a crawler is predicted. The Auto Regressive Integrated Moving Average, ARIMA(1,1,0) Model in time series analysis works well with the forecasting of time delay between the visits of search engine crawlers at Websites. 5 search engine crawlers are considered, all of which could be modeled using ARIMA(1,1,0). The Mean Square Error and Mean Forecast Error are very low and hence the two forecasting models are found acceptable. The result of this study is useful in predicting the server load.

Contents

Abstract 1

Contents 4

List of Figures 9

List of Tables 13

Chapter 1: Introduction 15

1.1 Types of Web Mining 18

1.2 Contents of Web Logs 20

    1.2 a) User's or Search Engine Crawler's IP Address 21

    1.2 b) User's Authentication Name 21

    1.2 c) Date-time Stamp of the Access 22

    1.2 d) HTTP Request 22

    1.2 e) Uniform Resource Locator (URL) Requested 22

    1.2 f) Protocol Version 22

    1.2 g) Response Status 22

    1.2 h) Size of the Requested File 23

    1.2 i) Referrer URL 23

    1.2 j) Browser and its Version 23

    1.2 k) Operating System and its Version 24

    1.2 l) Cookie Information 24

1.3 Need for Pre-Processing 24

1.4 Pre-processing Tasks 26

1.5 Applications of Web Usage Mining (Web Log Mining) 28

    1.5 a) Adaptive Websites 28

    1.5 b) Personalization of Websites 29

    1.5 c) Restructuring of Complex Websites 29

    1.5 d) Building Recommendation Systems 30

    1.5 e) Understanding User Preferences 31

    1.5 f) Management Decision Making 31

    1.5 g) Technology Management 32

    1.5 h) Assessing the Quality of Websites 32

    1.5 i) Analysis of the Violation of Intellectual Property Protection 32

    1.5 j) Predicting Future Requests 33

    1.5 k) Mining Association Rules 33

    1.5 l) Frequent Pattern Mining 33

    1.5 m) Pre-fetching and caching 34

    1.5 n) Analysis of Web server performance 35

    1.5 o) Analysis of Search Engine Crawler Behavior 36

    1.5 p) Forecasting of Search Engine Crawler Behavior 36

1.6 Thesis Organization and Framework 37

1.7 Test Data Sets 40

Chapter 2: Pre-processing of Web Logs and Web Usage Analytics 41

2.1 Pre-processing of Web Logs 41

    2.1.1 Indiscernibility Relations in Rough Set Theory 42

    2.1.2 Construction of Equivalence Classes from Web Logs 44

    2.1.3 User and Session Identification 47

    2.1.4 Pre-fetching and Caching 48

2.2 Web Usage Analytics 51

    2.2.1 Origin of Visits and Referring Sites 55

    2.2.2 Keywords 57

    2.2.3 User Agents 58

2.3 Conclusion 63

2.4 Publications based on this Chapter 64

Chapter 3: Clustering of Users and User Sessions 65

3.1 Background Literature 65

3.2 Deep Linking 69

3.3 Algorithm for Clustering Users based on *Entry Pages* 69

3.4 Results of Clustering Users based on *Entry Pages* 71

3.5 Algorithm for Clustering User Sessions based on *Entry Pages* 76

3.6 Results of Clustering User Sessions based on *Entry Pages* 79

3.7 Conclusion 81

3.8 Publications based on this Chapter 82

Chapter 4: Discovery of User Behavior 83

4.1 Analysis of Sequence Length 83

    4.1.1 Background Literature 83

    4.1.2 Methodology 84

    4.1.3 Sequence Length from Entry Point (Case I) 85

    4.1.4 Sequence Length of Repeated Visits (Case II) 88

4.2 Content and Navigational Pages 91

    4.2.1 Background Literature 91

    4.2.2 Rough Set Theory 93

    4.2.3 Identifying Content and Navigational Pages 95

    4.2.4 Temporal Analysis of Content and Navigational Pages..............103

4.3 Conclusion 104

4.4 Publications based on this Chapter 106

Chapter 5: Identification of Search Engine Crawler Behavior 107

5.1 Introduction..107

5.2 Background Literature 111

5.3 Pre-processing 115

5.4 Identification of Search Engine Crawlers and Visits................................116

5.5 Identification of Pages Crawled 123

    5.5.1 Kruskal Wallis H Test..125

5.6 Discovery of Temporal Behavior 128

5.7 Discovery of Time Delay 140

    5.7.1 Analysis of Variance (ANOVA) 141

    5.7.2 Duncan's Multiple Range Test 144

5.8 Conclusion 145

5.9 Publications based on this Chapter 147

Chapter 6: Forecasting of Search Engine Crawler Behavior 148

6.1 Background Literature 148

6.2 Forecasting of the Pages Crawled...150

    6.2.1 Forecasting Models 151

    6.2.2 Single Exponential Smoothing Method 154

6.3 Forecasting of Time Delay 158

    6.3.1 Model Identification 158

    6.3.2 Autocorrelation Function (ACF) and Partial Autocorrelation Function (PACF) 160

    6.3.3 Auto Regressive Integrated Moving Average Model (ARIMA) 166

6.4 Conclusion 170

6.5 Publications based on this Chapter 171

Chapter 7: Conclusion and Scope for Future Work 172

7.1 Conclusion 172

7.2 Scope for Future Work 176

Acknowledgements 178

References 179

List of Publications evolved out of this Thesis 203

Appendix 206

List of Figures

Fig. 1.1	Taxonomy of Web Mining	18
Fig. 1.2	Web Usage Mining Process	20
Fig. 1.3	Sample Web Log in Extended Log File Format	21
Fig. 1.4	Pre-processing tasks	26
Fig. 1.5	Thesis Framework	37
Fig. 2.1	Process Flow Diagram for generating Equivalence Classes from Web logs for successful user requests	46
Fig. 2.2	Input File for generation of Equivalence Classes for successful user requests	47
Fig. 2.3	Cleaned Web Log in Extended Log Format	47
Fig. 2.4	Process Flow Diagram for pre-processing of Web logs for pre-fetching and caching	50
Fig. 2.5	Results of pre-processing for pre-fetching and caching	51
Fig. 2.6	Process Flow Diagram for extracting origin of visits, referrer pages and keywords used to arrive at a Website	54
Fig. 2.7	Origin of visits and the percentage for data set 1	55
Fig. 2.8	Origin of visits and the percentage for data set 2	56
Fig. 2.9	Process Flow Diagram for extracting browsers and operating system	60
Fig. 3.1	Process of clustering users based on *Entry Pages*	70
Fig. 3.2	Process Flow Diagram for clustering users based on *Entry Pages*	71
Fig. 3.3	Percentage of visitors entered through Home page and other pages for data set 1	74
Fig. 3.4	Percentage of visitors entered through Home page and other pages for data set 2	74
Fig. 3.5	Percentage of Traffic through *Top Entry Pages* excluding Home page for data set 1	75

Fig. 3.6	Percentage of Traffic through *Top Entry Pages* excluding Home page for data set 2	75
Fig. 3.8	Process Flow Diagram for Rank Order Clustering of user sessions	78
Fig. 3.7	User session-page incidence matrix	79
Fig. 3.9	Results of final iteration	79
Fig. 3.10	Graphical representation of *Top Ten Entry Pages*, the similar and dissimilar user sessions for data set 1	80
Fig. 3.11	Graphical representation of *Top Ten Entry Pages*, the similar and dissimilar user sessions for data set 2	80
Fig. 4.1	Temporal information of mean sequence length of users entered through Home page and other pages for data set 1	87
Fig. 4.2	Temporal information of mean sequence length of users entered through Home page and other pages for data set 2	88
Fig. 4.3	Temporal information of mean sequence length of single visit and repeated visits for data set 1	90
Fig. 4.4	Temporal information of mean sequence length of single visit and repeated visits for data set 2	91
Fig. 4.5	Rough set concept with lower approximation, upper approximation and boundary regions of X	95
Fig. 4.6	Process Flow Diagram for identifying content and navigational pages	98
Fig. 4.7	Graphical representation of content and navigational pages for data set 1	99
Fig. 4.8	Graphical representation of content and navigational pages for data set 2	100
Fig. 5.1	Tasks involved in identification of search engine crawler behavior	117
Fig. 5.2	Time series sequence plot for data set 1	127
Fig. 5.3	Time series sequence plot for data set 2	128

Fig. 5.4	Time distribution for Baiduspider in data set 1	132
Fig. 5.5	Time distribution for Bingbot in data set 1	133
Fig. 5.6	Time distribution for Discobot in data set 1	133
Fig. 5.7	Time distribution for Ezooms in data set 1	134
Fig. 5.8	Time distribution for Feedfetcher-Google in data set 1	134
Fig. 5.9	Time distribution for Googlebot in data set 1	135
Fig. 5.10	Time distribution for Gosospider in data set 1	135
Fig. 5.11	Time distribution for Ichiro in data set 1	136
Fig. 5.12	Time distribution for MJ12bot in data set 1	136
Fig. 5.13	Time distribution for MSNbot in data set 1	137
Fig. 5.14	Time distribution for Slurp in data set 1	137
Fig. 5.15	Time distribution for Sogou in data set 1	138
Fig. 5.16	Time distribution for Sosospider in data set 1	138
Fig. 5.17	Time distribution for Yandex in data set 1	139
Fig. 5.18	Time distribution for Bingbot in data set 2	139
Fig. 5.19	Time distribution for Googlebot in data set 2	140
Fig. 5.20	Mean time plot of the time delay of various search engine crawlers in data set 1	144
Fig. 6.1	Horizontal pattern	152
Fig. 6.2	Trend pattern	152
Fig. 6.3	Seasonal pattern	153
Fig. 6.4	Cyclic pattern	153
Fig. 6.5	Observed and forecasted values for the number of pages crawled at Website 1	156
Fig. 6.6	Observed and forecasted values for the number of pages crawled at Website 2	156
Fig. 6.7	Box-Jenkin's model building process	159
Fig. 6.8	ACF for Baiduspider	161

Fig. 6.9	PACF for Baiduspider	161
Fig. 6.10	ACF for Bingbot	162
Fig. 6.11	PACF for Bingbot	163
Fig. 6.12	ACF for Feedfetcher-Google	163
Fig. 6.13	PACF for Feedfetcher-Google	164
Fig. 6.14	ACF for Googlebot	164
Fig. 6.15	PACF for Googlebot	165
Fig. 6.16	ACF for Slurp	165
Fig. 6.17	PACF for Slurp	166
Fig. 6.18	Observed and forecasted values of time delay between two consecutive visits for Baiduspider	168
Fig. 6.19	Observed and forecasted values of time delay between two consecutive visits for Bingbot	168
Fig. 6.20	Observed and forecasted values of time delay between two consecutive visits for Feedfetcher-Google	169
Fig. 6.21	Observed and forecasted values of time delay between two consecutive visits for Googlebot	169
Fig. 6.22	Observed and forecasted values of time delay between two consecutive visits for Slurp	170
Fig. A.1	Web log of business organization NeST ranging from January 1, 2011 to May 31, 2011	206
Fig. A.2	Web log of academic institution BPC College ranging from November 1, 2012 to December 31, 2012	207

List of Tables

Table 2.1	Status Codes of Hyper Text Transfer Protocol	42
Table 2.2	Statistics of Web log data before and after pre-processing for data set 1	48
Table 2.3	Statistics of Web log data before and after pre-processing for data set 2	48
Table 2.4	Percentage of users from top referring sites for data set 1	56
Table 2.5	Percentage of users from top referring sites for data set 2	57
Table 2.6	Frequent keywords used to access Website 1	58
Table 2.7	Frequent keywords used to access Website 2	58
Table 2.8	Statistics of different browsers and its version used by visitors in data set 1	61
Table 2.9	Statistics of different browsers and its version used by visitors in data set 2	61
Table 2.10	Statistics of various operating systems and its version found in data set 1	62
Table 2.11	Statistics of various operating systems and its version found in data set 2	62
Table 3.1	Number of clusters (*Entry Pages*) for data set 1	72
Table 3.2	Number of clusters (*Entry Pages*) for data set 2	72
Table 3.3	*Top Ten Entry Pages* and the percentage of traffic for data set 1	72
Table 3.4	*Top Ten Entry Pages* and the percentage of traffic for data set 2	73
Table 3.5	Statistics of *Entry Pages* and user sessions for data set 1 and data set 2	76
Table 3.6	*Top Ten Entry Pages*, the total and similar user sessions for data set 1	81
Table 3.7	*Top Ten Entry Pages*, the total and similar user sessions for data set 2	81
Table 4.1	Parameters for testing the mean sequence length of visitors through Home page and other pages for data set 1	86

Table 4.2	Parameters for testing the mean sequence length of visitors through Home page and other pages for data set 2	87
Table 4.3	Parameters for testing the mean sequence length of users with single visit and repeated visits for data set 1	89
Table 4.4	Parameters for testing the mean sequence length of users with single visit and repeated visits for data set 2	89
Table 4.5	Results of rough set approach for identifying content and navigational pages for data set 1	99
Table 4.6	Results of rough set approach for identifying content and navigational pages for data set 2	99
Table 4.7	Pages in lower approximation (content pages) for data set 1	101
Table 4.8	Pages in upper approximation (content and navigational pages) for data set 1	101
Table 4.9	Pages in lower approximation (content pages) for data set 2	102
Table 4.10	Pages in upper approximation (content and navigational pages) for data set 2	103
Table 4.11	Temporal analysis of the pages in lower approximation (content pages) for data set 1	104
Table 4.12	Temporal analysis of the pages in lower approximation (content pages) for data set 2	104
Table 5.1	Prominent crawlers identified in each data set and their description	118
Table 5.2	No: of visits by various crawlers for data set 1	122
Table 5.3	No: of visits by various crawlers for data set 2	123
Table 5.4	No: of pages crawled by various crawlers for data set 1	124
Table 5.5	No: of pages crawled by various crawlers for data set 2	125
Table 5.6	Test statistic for Case I	126
Table 5.7	Test statistic for Case II	127
Table 5.8	Results of pre-processing	129

Table 5.9	Total time spent in seconds by various search engine crawlers in data set 1	130
Table 5.10	Total time spent in seconds by various search engine crawlers in data set 2	131
Table 5.11	Test statistic	132
Table 5.12	Results of pre-processing	141
Table 5.13	Formula Summary for ANOVA	142
Table 5.14	Statistic descriptive of the time delay in seconds between visits of search engine crawlers in data set 1	143
Table 5.15	Results of One Way ANOVA	143
Table 5.16	Results of Duncan's Multiple Range Test	145
Table 6.1	Results of normalization and exponential smoothed forecasts	157

Acknowledgement

This research work is funded by Kerala State Council for Science Technology and Environment, Thiruvananthapuram, Kerala State, India as per order No.009/SRSPS/2011/CSTE.

Chapter 1: Introduction

World Wide Web has evolved in the last two decades with a tremendous growth in content on the Web and the number of users or visitors accessing the Web. In addition to users, the commercial search engine crawlers are also making their imprints on the Websites regularly. This growth is expected to follow in the years to come and many new innovations are taking place on the Web day by day. The increase in the growth of Web has given rise to a new branch of research known as Web Mining. This branch of research explores interesting information about the contents of Web page, the retrieval of information from Web, potential patterns in accessing the Web, Web page linkages and resources of E-commerce by using techniques of data mining. This may help to extract knowledge from the Web, improve Website design, and develop E-commerce better [[1]Liu01]. According to [[2]Kosala01], Web Mining tasks can be decomposed into following four sectors.

a) Resource Finding (Information Retrieval)

Resource finding is the process of retrieving data that is either online or offline from sources such as electronic newsletters, newsgroups, contents of HTML documents etc. The challenge is to automatically extract information without human intervention. The primary goal of Information Retrieval is to index text and search for useful documents in a collection.

b) Information Selection and Pre-processing

Information selection and pre-processing is any kind of transformation process of original data retrieved in the Information Retrieval process. Pre-processing is aimed at obtaining the desired representation or removal of irrelevant information from data. The data undergoes a transformation process in pre-processing.

c) Generalization

Generalization automatically discovers general patterns at individual Websites as well as across multiple Websites. This involves the use of machine learning and data mining techniques.

d) Analysis

Analysis focuses on validation and/or interpretation of the mined patterns. This is important in knowledge discovery and involves the use of visual tools. Since Web is an interactive medium, humans play an important role in analysis.

1.1 Types of Web Mining

The Web Mining can be broadly categorized into

    a) Web Content Mining
    b) Web Structure Mining
    c) Web Usage Mining or Web Log Mining [3Facca04][36Han08].

A taxonomy of Web Mining is proposed in various research works and is depicted in Fig. 1.1 [5Costa05] [8SenthilKumar08] [9Yu11] [10Malik10] [12Li02] [13Lappas08].

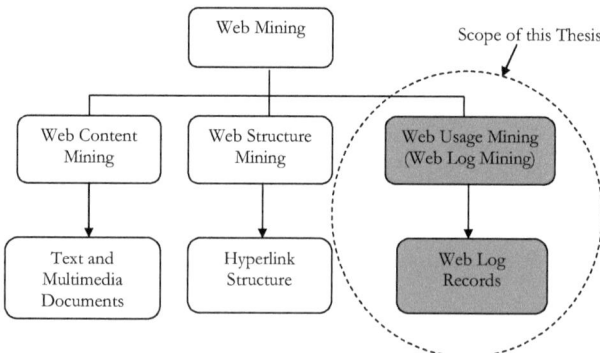

Fig. 1.1 Taxonomy of Web Mining

Web Content Mining is that part of Web Mining which focuses on the raw information available in Web. Web Content Mining targets the knowledge discovery, in which the main objects are traditional collections of text documents and more recently, the collections of multimedia documents such as images, videos and audios which are embedded in or linked to the Web pages [[7]Jicheng99][[4]Zhang08].

Web Structure Mining is that part of Web Mining which focuses on the structure of Websites. The source data for Web Structure Mining mainly consists of structural information present in Web pages (e.g. links to other pages). Typical applications include link-based categorization of Web pages, ranking of Web pages through a combination of content as well as structure and reverse engineering of Website models [[5]Costa05].

Web Usage Mining (Web Log Mining) is that part of Web Mining which deals with extraction of knowledge from server log files. Web Usage Mining is aimed to analyze the behavior of users as well as search engine crawlers visiting the Websites. The source data for Web Usage Mining mainly consists of (textual) logs that are collected when users access Web servers [[6]Cooley99]. While the Web Content and Structure mining utilize the primary data on Web, Web Usage Mining mines the secondary data derived from interactions of users or search engine crawlers while interacting with the Web. The Web usage data includes the data from browser logs (client logs) proxy server logs, Web server access logs, user profiles, registration data, user sessions or transactions, cookies, user queries, bookmark data, mouse clicks or scrolls and any other data as a result of interactions with Websites [[11]Sivaramakrishnan09].

The Web log files also contain traces of search engine crawlers which visited the Websites. Crawlers also known as 'bots', 'robots' or 'spiders' are highly automated programs sent by various search engines to periodically visit the World Wide Web and update contents on Web pages [[163]Giles10]. The traces left by the crawlers will be recorded in the Web log. This information plays a vital role in identifying the behavior of crawlers, the ethics of search engines, the server load, the dynamics of crawling and many more. Fig.1.2 illustrates a high level Web Usage Mining Process.

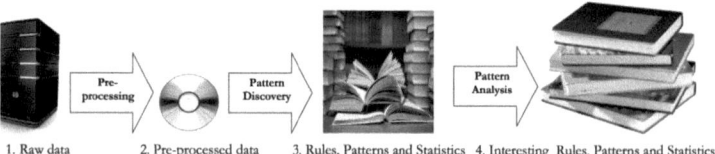

1. Raw data   2. Pre-processed data   3. Rules, Patterns and Statistics   4. Interesting Rules, Patterns and Statistics

Fig. 1.2 Web Usage Mining Process

1.2 Contents of Web Logs

Web logs are maintained by Web servers and contain information about users accessing the Website. Logs are mostly stored as simple text files which are highly unstructured. The most widely used log file formats are Common Log File Format and Extended Log File Format [16Spiliopoulou00] [14Grcar04] [15Wahab08]. Traditionally there are four types of server logs namely Transfer log, Agent log, Error log and Referrer log [17Bertot97].The referrer and agent logs may or may not be turned on at the server or may be added to the transfer log file to create an Extended Log File Format. There are three main sources to get the raw Web log file [18Hussain10]. They are

a) Client log file
b) Proxy log file
c) Server log file.

Client log files are most accurate and authentic to depict the user behavior but it is a difficult task to modify the browser for each client. In proxy servers, same IP address is used by many users. Hence to identify users is a challenging task. Most researchers consider the Web server log file as most reliable and accurate for Web Usage Mining process. Fig. 1.3 shows a sample Web log in Extended Log File Format.

```
4.125.112.80 - - [01/Apr/2011:00:01:23 +051800] "GET / HTTP/1.1" 200 51357 "-" "Feedfetcher-Google; (+http://www.goo   } Record 1
gle.com/feedfetcher.html; feed-id=17021125084900405113)"
119.63.196.100 - - [01/Apr/2011:00:02:39 +051800] "GET /index.php?Itemid=28&id=26&option=com_content&task=view        } Record 2
HTTP/1.1" 200 41255 "-" "Mozilla/5.0 (compatible; Baiduspider/2.0; +http://www.baidu.com/search/spider.html)"
crawl-66-249-67-241.googlebot.com - - [01/Apr/2011:00:02:54 +051800] "GET /robots.txt HTTP/1.1" 200 286 "-" "Mozilla/5.0 } Record 3
(compatible; Googlebot/2.1; +http://www.google.com/bot.html)"
crawl-66-249-67-241.googlebot.com - - [01/Apr/2011:00:03:04 +051800] "GET /index.php?option=com_search&searchword=     } Record 4
fib HTTP/1.1" 200 65648 "-" "Mozilla/5.0 (compatible; Googlebot/2.1; +http://www.google.com/bot.html)"
crawl-66-249-67-241.googlebot.com - - [01/Apr/2011:00:09:17 +051800] "GET /index.php?option=com_
search&Itemid=99999999&searchword=chnology&searchphrase=any&ordering=newest&limit=5&limitstart=25 HTTP/1.1" 200        } Record 5
51105 "-" "Mozilla/5.0 (compatible; Googlebot/2.1; +http://www.google.com/bot.html)"
```

Fig. 1.3 Sample Web Log in Extended Log File Format

The Extended Web log [20Woon02] [21Aye11] [22Ciesielski03] [23Lu03] [24Joshi03] [25Haigh98] [26Zaiane01] contains the following information and is used for analysis throughout the thesis.

1.2 a) User's or Search Engine Crawler's IP Address

Client IP (User IP) is the Internet Protocol address of computer who access or request the Website. The Website may be accessed by a user or a search engine crawler.

1.2 b) User's Authentication Name

Some Websites are set up with a security feature that requires a user to enter username and password. Once a user logs on to a Website, that user's "username" is recorded in the log file. If no user authentication is required, a "-" will appear in the log file.

1.2 c) Date-time Stamp of the Access

The date and time stamp shows the date and time at which a particular page is accessed. It is recorded for each hit. The date format is DD-MM-YYYY. The time format is HH:MM:SS. It also has a component to show how many seconds the time differs from Greenwich Mean Time (GMT).

1.2 d) HTTP Request

Usually there are four ways of HTTP requests namely PUT, GET, POST and HEAD which are found in Web logs. PUT method replaces all current representations of the target resource with the uploaded content. The GET method is used to retrieve information from the given server using a given Uniform Resource Locator. A POST request is used to send data to the server. For example, the customer information, file upload etc using HTML forms are done using POST. HEAD is similar to GET, but only transfer the status line and header section. Most HTML files are served via GET method while CGI functionality is served via POST or HEAD.

1.2 e) Uniform Resource Locator (URL) Requested

It shows the actual path of the page requested. URL query usually appears after sign "?". This represents the type of user request and the value appears in the address bar.

1.2 f) Protocol Version

It shows the protocol version of HTTP used like HTTP 1.0 or HTTP 1.1

1.2 g) Response Status

This is the status code returned by the server which will be a three digit number. There are four classes of codes:

i. Success (200 series)
ii. Redirect (300 series)
iii. Failure (400 series)
iv. Server Error (500 series)

A status code of 200 means the transaction was successful. Common 300 series codes are 301 for Web pages moved permanently, 302 for Web pages moved temporarily etc. The most common failure codes are 401 for failed authentication, 403 for forbidden request to a restricted subdirectory and 404 for file not found messages. The most common 500 series codes are 500 for server error, 504 for gateway time out and 505 for HTTP version not supported. The status code 200 is the only successful status code and other status codes like 300 series, 400 series, 500 series etc. are unsuccessful status codes. All records with unsuccessful status codes need to be eliminated while pre-processing. [19Pabarskaite07][28Suneetha09]. [27http://www.w3.org/protocols11] gives a list of various status codes of Hyper Text Transfer Protocol.

1.2 h) Size of the Requested File

This shows the amount of data sent by client to the server. It is represented in bytes.

1.2 i) Referrer URL

The referring page, if any, as reported by remote user's browser is recorded in the log file. It can be a page within a Website or other referring sites from which the request is originated.

1.2 j) Browser and its Version

The type of browser used to access a Website is also recorded in the log file. There are several different Web browsers on the market today (e.g.

Netscape, Microsoft Internet Explorer, Lynx, Mosaic, Chrome) each of which has different viewing capabilities. The different versions of various browsers used to access a Website are also recorded in the Web log.

1.2 k) Operating System and its Version

The type of operating system and its version used to access the Website is recorded in the Web log. (e.g. Windows XP, Windows 7, Ubuntu 9.04)

1.2 l) Cookie Information

A cookie is the term given to describe a type of message that is given to a Web browser by a Web server. The main purpose of a cookie is to identify users and possibly prepare customized Web pages. Cookie information is a token which defines the cookie sent to a visitor. These cookies can be used to track individual users and is helpful in generating sessions. But cookies raise the concern of privacy and require the co-operation of users.

Common Log File Format lacks the fields referrer URL, browser with its version, operating system with its version and cookie information. Hence Extended Log File Format provides more information than Common Log File Format about the users or search engine crawlers accessing a Website and is used for data analysis in the forthcoming Chapters.

1.3 Need for Pre-Processing

The analysis of log files poses a series of challenges. These files contain significant data for the Web Mining process but they also include a large amount of noise. Many of the challenges to deal with Web server log data can be resolved by properly architecting the E-commerce sites to generate data needed for mining [29Kohavi01]. The problems identified in log file processing are

a) The need for a large storage space due to considerable volume of data saved on a disc. A busy server may generate log files in the order of few megabytes or terabytes for one single day.
b) The existence of a large amount of data that is irrelevant for the Web Usage Mining process, as a result of accessing the files containing images, JavaScripts, etc.
c) Storage of requests performed by search engines and various automated scripts.
d) The storage of data containing error messages, such as 300(redirects) 400(bad request), 500(internal server error) etc.
e) Prevention from real time data usage due to the batch processing of log files [30Mican09][31Zhang02].

Every time a Web browser downloads an HTML document from the internet, the images are also downloaded and stored in the log file. A *hit* is any file from a Website that a user downloads and *access* is an entire page downloaded by users regardless of the number of images, sounds or movies [32Burton01]. A *hit* can be a text document, image, movie or a sound file. For example, if a user downloads a Web page that has 6 images on it, then the number of *hits* is 7(1 text page + 6 images) whereas the user has accessed just one page of the Website. Most Web analysis software counts the number of *hits* a server receives rather than the number of *accesses*.

Search engine crawlers can generate 90% of the traffic on Websites [30Mican09]. The robots contain specific codes that are able to capture a wider range of IP addresses. Such string examples can be 'Google' or 'Googlebot' for Google search engine, 'Yahoo' or 'Slurp' for Yahoo search engine, 'MSNbot' for MSN, 'spider' for Sosospider and so on. The IPs containing any of the above mentioned substrings can be identified as a search engine visit and hence eliminated. Similarly the 'robots.txt' in the URL requested field and strings like 'bot', 'spider', 'crawl' etc. in the browser field are also requests from the search engines. In order to assure that data contain only useful information for the users, it is absolutely necessary for the log files to be cleaned and filtered. Similarly when the behavior of search engine crawlers is studied the tasks to be performed are

a) Removal of all user related information
b) Removal of unsuccessful requests from search engine crawlers

While analyzing the user behavior, the search engine crawler's requests need to be eliminated and while studying the behavior of search engine crawlers, the user requests should be eliminated. Otherwise it may bias the data mining tasks to follow.

1.4 Pre-processing Tasks

The pre-processing tasks are shown in Fig 1.4. The first pre-processing task is data cleaning. The process of data cleaning is to remove noise or irrelevant data. Web logs do not automatically identify a user or a visitor [33Pitkow97]. Each user can be identified by the IP address, cookies, logins, path analysis and user agents like browser or operating system [34Catledge95].

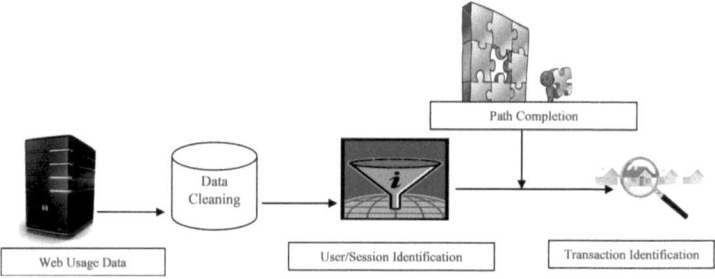

Fig. 1.4 Pre-processing tasks

The main data pre-processing tasks involve identification of users, user sessions, path completion and transaction identification. A session timeout of 25.5 minutes is used by [34Catledge95]. A 30 minute time window is used in [35Srivastava00] for identifying user sessions. This is followed in many of the literature available to identify user sessions [37Suresh06][38Aghabozorgi09][39Raju08][42Thakare10][43Zheng10].

Path completion is necessary to be carried out due to the existence of local caching and proxy servers. The user access paths are incompletely preserved in the Web access log. If the hyperlink between the current request page and a page next to the last request does not exist, then the path is incomplete and needs to be added. To discover user's travel pattern, the missing pages in user access paths should be appended. [130Munk10] specifies the reconstruction of activities of a Web visitor. For different mining tasks, user access paths should be distinguished as different kinds of transactions.

There are three methods for transaction identification namely Reference Length, Maximal Forward Reference and Time Window [6Cooley99][40Peng09]. To find out the user's travel patterns and user's interests in Web Usage Mining, two kinds of transactions are necessary to be defined, i.e. travel-path transactions and content-only transactions. The travel-path transaction consists of both content and auxiliary pages. It indicates the sequence of user's accessed pages. Mining these travel-path transactions would essentially give the common traversal paths of a user. The content-only transaction is defined as all content pages of a user session. Mining these content-only transactions will discover the users' interests and cluster users visiting the Website [41Li09]. Web log data can be represented using tree structured Web log data representation [99Hadzicand11].[126Snyder09] demonstrate a method for estimating values for missing portions of time sensitive DNS log data. This method would be suitable for use with a variety of data sets containing time series values where certain portions are missing.

1.5 Applications of Web Usage Mining (Web Log Mining)

There are several potential and diverse applications for Web Log Mining. With the advent of World Wide Web, E-commerce, E-governance, E-learning and E-business have flourished through their Websites. Web logs contain tremendous information about the behavior of users and search engine crawlers visiting a Website. Web users have different purposes and intentions when browsing a Website. Each user's intention and purpose can be determined by an inspection of their browsing activities. By tracking interactive user behavior, the system can help designers detect user access patterns and can suggest ways to build more efficient Websites.

1.5 a) Adaptive Websites

[[44]Perkowitz00] propose adaptive Websites that automatically improve their organization and presentation by learning from visitor access patterns. Systems, which adapt themselves automatically to current user needs or perceived requirements and to his/her current task are called adaptive [[45]Lee04]. Adaptive Websites include customization which is adapting the site's presentation to the needs of each individual visitor based on information about those individuals. Any changes impact only that single user, effectively creating numerous versions of the site, one per user. It also takes care of the division of labor between the automated assistant and the human Web master. The program could be fully manual in which the Web master simply specifies the changes to be carried out. It can also be fully automated i.e., allowed to make changes to the Website on its own. Many programs will be semi-automated, requiring Web master approval to make limited kinds of alterations. More generally, adaptations could add or remove links, highlight links, change text or formatting and even create completely new Web pages.

1.5 b) Personalization of Websites

Adaptations can be done based on the content of pages or people's navigational choices. Web log analysis can also help build customized Web services for individual users. Based on clustering of user transactions and clustering of page views, overlapping aggregate profiles can be discovered and effectively used in building recommender systems for real-time Web personalization. [47Mobasher02] has used the generated aggregate profiles, for effective personalization at early stages of user's visits to a site, based only on anonymous click stream data and without the benefit of explicit input by these users or deeper knowledge about them. Finding information relevant to user needs has become increasingly important. [48Puntheeranurak05] have developed an approach that use information learned from user's Web log data to construct accurate comprehensive individual profiles [49Eirinaki03].

1.5 c) Restructuring of Complex Websites

Another application of Web Usage Mining is restructuring of complex Websites [61Chou02]. Similar to the engineering processes of any type of complex product life-cycle from software to an automobile, usability techniques and processes involve testing and quantitative evaluation. Incorporating usability techniques in the redesign process of a large and complex Website is yet another application of Web Usage Mining. A solid Website architecture design increases usability. Ease to find an information or infrastructure and information design, connects users to content by managing information in a logical and organized fashion. In short, information architecture provides a strategy and a way of labeling content to manage information.

1.5 d) Building Recommendation Systems

[51Flesca05] has proposed an approach for personalizing Website navigation based on a combination of knowledge raised from the field of recommendation systems with Web Usage and Content Mining techniques. User browsing preferences and usage/content relatedness among Web pages are exploited for supporting users in the navigation of a Website. The preferred browsing path is studied [64Jiang10] and is useful in online commercial activities [65Dai06][67Yang10]. The recommendation technique accomplishes a major desirable feature which is effectively improving the user experience in accessing relevant contents available from a Website and at the same time, maintaining the original structure and content organization of the Website [52Zhang07] [70Peng08]. Since Web log data provides information about specific page's popularity and the methods used to access them, this information can be integrated with Web Content and Structure Mining to help rank Web pages, classify Web documents and construct a multilayered Web information base[46Han02][53Velasquez03].

Web Usage Mining techniques also play an important role in E-commerce and E-services. It provides useful tools for understanding how E-commerce and E-service Websites and services are being used, enabling the provision of better services for customers and users [54Ting08][57Zhang10]. Personalized recommendation in E-commerce is a personalized service that a user can enjoy when visiting a Website. For e.g. certain Websites like amazon.com provides personalized recommendation while purchasing books. When a book is added to the cart, it provides recommendation of similar books or books with related subjects. The Website recommends some online pages potentially interesting to the user according to the clustering features [50Cho02]. The E-commercial recommendation system by [58Lian11] uses collaborative filtering technology in mining Web logs. Collaborative clustering can effectively increase the real-time response speed of recommendation algorithm. To realize online page recommendation, the recommendation algorithm uses page weight in user cluster and user's average evaluation on page as two recommendation factors.

1.5 e) Understanding User Preferences

[[60]Mena01] has done a case study concerned with an Internet radio station striving to become more intelligent about their visitors which is another application of Web Log Mining. Visitors were identified as heavy listeners, light listeners and non-listeners.

1.5 f) Management Decision Making

The process of analyzing large data sets in order to find patterns that can help to isolate key variables to build predictive models for management decision making is another application of Web Log Mining. This is termed as business intelligence [[55]Lau04]. What differentiate companies in today's highly competitive markets is their ability to make accurate, timely and effective decisions at all levels – operational, tactical and strategic to address their customer's dynamic preferences and priorities. Increasingly, companies around the globe have started using advanced (also known as predictive) analytics to analyze their data (both structured and unstructured), combining information on past circumstances, present events and projected future actions. By incorporating advanced analytics into their daily operations, these organizations gain control over the decisions they make every day so that they can successfully meet their business goals. The insight that they gain from such analysis is then used to direct, optimize and automate their decision making. It results in successful achievement of a variety of specific organizational goals, whether they are associated with an increase in cross-sell revenue generation, a decrease in production or service cost, a reduction in fraudulent behavior or an increase in promotional campaign response rates [56Bose09]. The Web log data of user's feedback can be used and data mining can be applied to build the user space to improve the retrieval performance [66Yijun02].

1.5 g) Technology Management

Web Usage Mining is an evolving discipline and it has remarkable contributions on the data gathering and processing of the abundant non-structural data at network age. Scientists, technological administrators and policymakers are all full of interests in its applications in future. The application of Web Log Mining for technology management includes information searching and gathering for obtaining the necessary data from Web, to identify the technology subject/relationship, analysis of technology opportunities, behavioral daily record etc. [59Chengjian08].

1.5 h) Assessing the Quality of Websites

Assessing the quality of Websites is yet another application of Web Usage Mining [62Ruddle09] [63Hasan11]. It includes usability factors like easy to use, understand, navigate, reliability factors like availability of the Web pages, multi-browser support etc. and customization factor like tailoring content to the need of specific users. All these factors could be studied by mining Web logs.

1.5 i) Analysis of the Violation of Intellectual Property Protection

Web Log Mining has also found application in analyzing the violation of intellectual property protection [68Jose10]. Websites are considered as one's intellectual property in cyberspace. Users may access a Website without visiting the Home page. While user performs searches in a search engine, some inner pages will be displayed and users may enter into the Websites through these inner pages without visiting the Home page. Cyber law experts consider this as a violation of intellectual property protection. These violations could be studied by mining the Web logs.

1.5 j) Predicting Future Requests

Mining Web logs can be used in predicting user's future requests [[69]Liu07][[71]Shyu06]. This is helpful in association rule mining, collaborative filtering, recommendation systems and customization of Web pages. An n-gram-based prediction algorithm that can predict future Web requests is developed by [[85]Yang03].

1.5 k) Mining Association Rules

Another application of Web Log Mining is to mine association rules. This is useful in the market basket analysis of various online portals to see which all pages are visited together in a single session. The association rule mining aids in the discovery of interesting relationships among huge amounts of Web log data which is particularly helpful in many decision making process, cross-selling, up-selling and customer shopping behavior analysis. Apriori algorithm to mine association rules was first proposed by [[72]Agrawal94]. Rough set theory can be applied to mine maximal association rules [[73]Guan03][[74]Hu06][[75]Liu08].

1.5 l) Frequent Pattern Mining

While the association rule mining does not take into consideration, the order of Web pages mined, frequent pattern mining considers the order of pages accessed [[76]Han07]. Mining frequent sequential patterns of multidimensional nature from any Web server log file leads to obtain the frequent Web access patterns [[77]Vijayalakshmi09]. To gain the competitive advantage in today's age of technology, growing data and to bear the competitive pressure, making strong decisions according to customer's need and market trend has become very important. With huge amount of data on internet, Web Usage Mining has become very significant. Frequent patterns help companies to produce productive information pertaining to the future of their business function ability by analyzing the usage information from their Websites. Sequential patterns allow the collection of Web access data for pages. This usage data provides the paths leading to accessed Web pages and their sequences which can give us valuable information about user's behavior and effectiveness of Websites [78Sajid10]. Initially obtaining a set of frequent access patterns and then using the combination of frequent access patterns and Website topology to discover new patterns will provide valuable data for the Website construction [79Peng10]. Frequent sequential pattern mining has another application. It is to find pages that are accessed together by majority of the users and hence should be linked in a proper way to maximize user satisfaction by providing the access flow they expect [80Nagi11]. Developing sequential classifiers for predicting user's next visits based on current actions using association rule mining is yet another application of Web Log Mining [113Yang03].

1.5 m) Pre-fetching and caching

Application of Web Log Mining includes pre-fetching and caching of most frequently accessed Web pages. Caching is done to improve the performance of Web servers. Pre-fetching and caching may improve latency time, reduces response time of a requested document but at the same time increases network load. Static caching is an application of Web Usage Mining. In static caching, the set of documents kept in the cache is determined periodically by analyzing log file for the previous period. The cache is filled with documents to maximize cache performance. Static caching incurs no CPU overhead and does not suffer from any memory fragmentation [81Tatarinov97].

1.5 n) Analysis of Web server performance

Another application of Web Log Mining is for the analysis of Web server performance. Web server performance is a critical issue for Websites which service a high volume of requests. This can be obtained by analyzing Web logs and performance data from several real Websites [82Iyengar97]. Intelligent Web caching is yet another application of Web Log Mining. It incorporates data warehousing of Web log data, extraction of data mining models and simulation of the Web caching algorithms, around an architecture that integrates the various phases in the knowledge discovery process [83Bonchi01]. Intelligent Web caching algorithms can also employ predictive models of Web requests [84Bonchi01] [93Sulaiman11]. Caching is a well known strategy for improving the performance of Web based systems. The heart of a caching system is its page replacement policy, which selects the pages to be replaced in a cache when a request arrives. Web Log Mining method for caching Web objects and can use this to enhance the performance of Web caching systems. Web pre-fetching techniques are especially important to reduce perceived Web latencies [87Domenech06] [92Domenech10]. Web logs can be mined to improve hit ratios of pre-fetching and caching [86Huang05]. In order to improve the quantitative measures such as hit ratios and byte hit ratios, a prediction-based buffer manager which takes appropriate actions such as document caching, document pre-fetching and can even adjust the buffer size could be developed.

Network congestion remains one of the main barriers to the continuing success of the internet. One possible remedy to the latency problem is to use caching at the client, at the proxy server or within the internet server. Caching at the client side can be done by analyzing the Web log. This could reduce the response time of a requested page [88Balamash07] [91Pallis08]. Although Web performance can be improved by caching, the benefit of using it is rather limited owing to filling the cache with documents without any prior knowledge. Web pre-fetching becomes an attractive solution when forthcoming page accesses of a client are predicted. This could be done by mining access log information [[89]Gulati08]. Pre-fetching becomes very popular to predict the possibility of which Web object could be requested in near future. The prediction for Web caching model, which apply Web Usage Mining and machine learning techniques for pre-fetching and caching is proposed by [[90]Songwattana08].

1.5 o) Analysis of Search Engine Crawler Behavior

Another important application of Web Log Mining is to study the behavior of search engine crawlers that periodically visit Websites for updating the contents of Web pages. The ethics of search engine crawlers can be studied to analyze the way the crawlers are accessing the Web pages [[162]Drott02][[163]Giles10]. The search engine traffic, the dynamicity of search engine crawlers which contributes to the server load can also be analyzed.

1.5 p) Forecasting of Search Engine Crawler Behavior

Forecasting of the behavior of search engine crawlers is important in analyzing the server load. E-commerce Websites are interested in predicting the user's behavior. There are few works in literature that forecasts the behavior of search engine crawlers. [[212]http://www.academia.edu/3252414/Coverage_and_Delay_Forecast_Modeling_of_Search_Engine_Services] has proposed forecasting models for service coverage and delay of search engines in the Australian government area using predictor variables, identified from the crawling policies of academic papers and statistical regression methods. The Logistic regression method was employed for coverage forecast and Poisson regression method for delay.

1.6 Thesis Organization and Framework

A Framework of this Thesis is given in Fig 1.5.

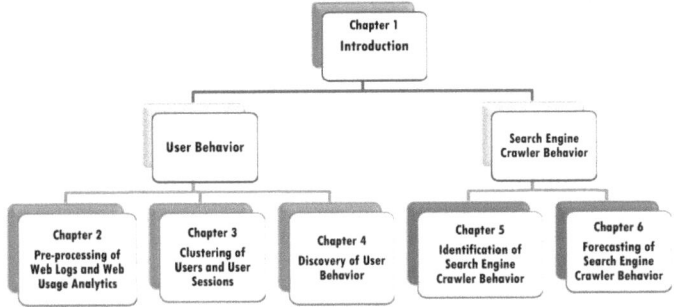

Fig. 1.5 Thesis Framework

Chapter 2 deals with pre-processing of Web logs and Web usage analytics. Web log data contains a large amount of noise and hence pre-processing is mandatory before any data mining functionality to follow. Two algorithms are proposed for pre-processing of Web log files based on indiscernibility relations in rough set theory which generates Equivalence Classes. The first algorithm generates a file with successful user requests while the second one generates a pre-processed file for pre-fetching and caching purposes. The pre-processed file for pre fetching and caching contains the frequently accessed Web pages with its frequency and total bytes transferred.

Two algorithms are proposed for usage analytics. The first algorithm identifies the origin of visits of users, the top referring sites and the most popular keywords used by the visitor to arrive at a Website. The second algorithm extracts the user agents which includes browsers (including version) and operating systems (including version) used by various visitors to arrive at a Website. It is important to know the origin of visitors for a Website developer, so that a better search engine optimization can be performed. The origin of visits is helpful in identifying how a user arrived at a Website (e.g. direct URL, referring sites or through search engines). Top referring Websites give information about the traffic from external Websites. Extraction of most popular keywords used by a visitor to arrive at a Website is helpful in meta-tag stuffing which results in better search engine rankings. The identification of user agents like browser with its version and operating system with its version provides information about the user agents(browsers and operating systems) used by visitors to access a Website. The absence of some popular browsers may due to the reason that the Website requires browser with specific viewing capabilities. Website designers can consider this while redesigning or restructuring the Website.

Chapter 3 proposes two algorithms. The first algorithm is for clustering users based on *Entry Pages*. It analyzes the deep linked traffic at a Website, percentage of traffic through *Top Ten Entry Pages* and temporal information of *Top Ten Entry pages*. Unlike traditional K-means, the number of clusters need not be given as input. The deep linked traffic may rethink the organization's policy of placing the advertisements on the Home page without considering the traffic through other pages.

The second algorithm is a Rank Order Clustering algorithm to identify similar user sessions from the *Entry Pages* to a Website. User sessions are consecutive pages visited by a user in a single session. This information is vital in frequent pattern mining, association rule mining, market-basket analysis, pre-fetching of frequently accessed Web pages, caching of Web pages and building recommender systems.

Chapter 4 contributes to the user behavior. It deals with analysis of sequence length of visitors, the depth to which a user visits a Website. An analytical study is done to identify the sequence length from the entry point to a Website. It is found that the mean sequence length of visitors entered through

Home page is higher than the mean sequence length of visitors entered through other pages. The mean sequence length of visitors with single visit and mean sequence length of repeated visitors is also analyzed. It is found that sequence length decreases in repeated visits. In case of repeated visits, the visitors may be familiar with the Website architecture and may be accessing only the required pages.

Another contribution of this Chapter is the identification of content and navigational pages in a Website using rough set approach. Content pages are those pages in which user stay for a long time. Navigational pages are those pages which act as link to other pages. A temporal analysis of the content and navigational pages is done to see whether the properties of the pages change with time. Identification of content and navigational pages is useful in target advertising.

Chapter 5 discovers the behavior of search engine crawlers. It includes identification of various search engine crawlers, identification of their behavior in terms of visits, pages crawled and identification of temporal behavior. It is found that there is a significant difference in the number of visits, pages crawled, time spent and time delay between two consecutive visits by various search engine crawlers. Kruskal Wallis H Test, Analysis of Variance (ANOVA) and Duncan's Multiple Range Test are used. The results revealed that there is a significant difference in the number of visits, pages crawled, time spent and time delay between two consecutive visits of search engine crawlers. This finding is helpful in studying the dynamicity of the crawlers, calculating the server load and ethics of search engine crawlers accessing the Websites. The more the number of crawlers is accessing a Website, the more will be the visibility of Websites.

Chapter 6 focuses on the forecasting of the behavior of search engine crawlers. A forecasting model for predicting the number of pages crawled by search engine crawlers is proposed. Single Exponential Smoothing method is used to build the forecasting model. The observed and forecasted values showed that this model is acceptable. Another forecasting model Auto

Regressive Integrated Moving Average ARIMA(1,1,0) is proposed for forecasting the time delay of search engine crawlers. Five search engine crawlers are selected for forecasting. The observed and predicted values revealed that this model works well with the prediction of search engine crawlers.

Chapter 7 concludes overall work in the above Chapters and discusses about the scope for future work in this area.

1.7 Test Data Sets

Two data sets are used for testing the proposed algorithms, statistical analysis and for testing the proposed forecasting models. The first data set is of a business organization NeST ranging from January 1, 2011 to May 31, 2011 (Appendix Fig. A.1). The second data set is of an academic institution BPC College, Kerala, India ranging from November 1, 2012 to December 31, 2012 (Appendix Fig. A.2).

>> *End of Chapter 1*<<

Chapter 2: Pre-processing of Web Logs and Web Usage Analytics

Web Usage Mining needs tremendous amount of pre-processing before any data mining functionality to follow. The pre-processing will remove irrelevant records which otherwise may affect the mining results. This chapter is divided into 2 sections namely pre-processing of Web logs and Web usage analytics. Two pre-processing algorithms are proposed based on indiscernibility relations in rough set theory which generates Equivalence Classes. The first algorithm pre-processes the raw file for further identification of users and user sessions. The second algorithm pre-processes the log file and gives the pages accessed, its frequency and total bytes transferred. Two algorithms are proposed to extract usage analytics. The first algorithm identifies the origin of user visits, top referring sites and most popular keywords used by the visitor to arrive at a Website. The second algorithm extracts browsers with its version and operating system with its version used by various visitors to access a Website. The browser and operating system are together known as user agents. All algorithms are tested on two different data sets and the results are displayed.

2.1 Pre-processing of Web Logs

The need for pre-processing is explained in section 1.3. The advantages of pre-processing include the elimination of considerable amount of space needed to store irrelevant records and the precision of mining results can be improved. This Chapter deals with pre-processing of Web log files related to mine user behavior and hence all the search engine crawler requests, unsuccessful requests, other irrelevant requests containing .jpg, .mpg, .gif, .png, .txt, .wav etc. are removed. The indiscernibility relation in rough set theory is used for pre-processing [234 Jose12] [240 Jose12]. Table 2.1 shows various status codes of Hyper Text Transfer Protocol [27 http://www.w3.org/protocols11] indicating response status.

Table 2.1 Status Codes of Hyper Text Transfer Protocol

101	Switching Protocols	404	Not Found
200	OK	405	Method Not Allowed
201	Created	406	Not Acceptable
202	Accepted	407	Proxy Authentication Required
203	Non Authoritative Information	408	Request Time Out
204	No Content	409	Conflict
205	Reset Content	410	Gone
206	Partial Content	411	Length Required
300	Multiple Choices	412	Precondition Failed
301	Moved Permanently	413	Request Entity Too Large
302	Moved Temporarily	414	Request URL Too Large
303	See Other	415	Unsupported Media Type
304	Not Modified	500	Server Error
305	Use Proxy	501	Not Implemented
400	Bad Request	502	Bad Gateway
401	Unauthorized	503	Out of Resources
402	Payment Required	504	Gateway Time Out
403	Forbidden	505	HTTP Version not Supported

2.1.1 Indiscernibility Relations in Rough Set Theory

A rough set based feature selection for Web Usage Mining is used in [94Inbarani07]. The experimental result shows the importance of the Web data pre-processing and it reduces the size of the log file. Feature selection is a pre-processing step in data mining and is very effective in reducing dimensions. Feature selection process refers to choose a subset of attributes from the set of original attributes. The purpose of feature selection is to identify the significant features, eliminate the irrelevant of dispensable features to the learning task and build a good learning model. The indiscernibility relation in rough set theory is used for clustering in [95Hirano05]. The main advantage of this method is that it can be applied to proximity measures that do not satisfy the triangular inequality and very well handles relative proximity. Relative proximity is a class of proximity measures that is suitable for representing subjective similarity or dissimilarity such as the degree of likeness between people.

Indiscernibility relations in rough set theory [96Pawalak02] can be used for the data cleaning of Web log files. Rough set is based on the assumption that with every object of the universe of discourse, some information is associated. Objects characterized by the same information are indiscernible (similar) in view of the available information about them. Any set of all indiscernible (similar) objects is called an elementary set and forms a basic granule of knowledge about the universe. Any union of some elementary sets is referred to as crisp (precise) set otherwise the set is rough (imprecise, vague).

Let a given pair S= (U,A) of non–empty finite sets U and A, where U is the Universe of objects and A is the set consisting of attributes. The function a: U→ Va , where Va is the set of values of attribute a called the domain of a. The pair S=(U,A) is called an information system. Any information system can be represented by a data table with rows labeled by objects and columns labeled by attributes. Any pair (x, a) where x ϵ U and a ϵ A defines the table entry consisting of the value a(x). Any subset B of A determines a binary relation I(B) on U, called an indiscernibility relation defined by x I(B)y if and only if a(x)=a(y) for every a ϵ B, where a(x) denotes the value of attribute a for object x and I(B) is an Equivalence Relation. The family of all Equivalence Classes of I(B) will be denoted by U/I(B) or simply U/B. Equivalence Classes of the relation I(B) of the partition U/B are referred to as B-elementary sets or B-elementary granules[97Pawlak07]. Let U represents the set of all user sessions with the path traversed. Let A be the subset of U which represents the HTTP request, URL requested and status code (response status). An indiscernibility relation I(B) is defined for every a(x)=a(y).

2.1.2 Construction of Equivalence Classes from Web Logs

The subset of Web log file entry which includes <HTTP request, URL requested, status code> is considered for indiscernibility relation and is denoted by B. Based on the values of these attributes, the family of all Equivalence Classes like <GET, *.html, 200>, <GET, *.php, 200>,<GET, *.aspx, 200>, <GET, *.jsp, 200>, <GET, *php*, 200>, <GET, */, 200>,<GET, *.html, 300>,<GET, *.gif, 200> ,<GET, *.jpg, 200>, <GET, *.txt, 200>, <GET, *.png, 200>, <GET, *.html, 404>, <GET, *.php, 404>, <GET, *.jsp, 404>, <GET *php*, 404>, <GET, *.wav, 200> etc. are generated and it is denoted as U(B) . Out of the Equivalence Classes generated, the indiscernibility relation having the attribute values<GET, *.html, 200>, <GET, *.php, 200>,<GET, *.aspx, 200>, <GET, *.jsp, 200>, <GET, *php*, 200> and <GET, */, 200> are the Equivalence Classes which is useful for further Web Usage Mining to follow. The advantage of this method is that all other Equivalence Classes generated can be further used to perform other statistical analysis like percentage of bad requests, mean number of redirects, percentage of reduction in the size of log file etc. Algorithm 2.1 shows the generation of Equivalence Classes from Web logs for successful user requests and Fig 2.1 shows the Process Flow Diagram for generating Equivalence Classes from Web logs for successful user requests. Fig. 2.2 shows the input file for generation of Equivalence Classes for successful user requests. The output of Algorithm 2.1, a cleaned Web log in Extended Log Format is shown in Fig. 2.3.

Input: A raw Web log file in Extended Log Format.

Output: Generated Equivalence Classes with values <GET, *.html, 200>, <GET, *.php, 200>,<GET, *.aspx, 200>, <GET, *.jsp, 200>, <GET, *php*, 200> and <GET, /, 200>.

Method:
```
Begin
    1. Extract the fields from a raw log file to a
    spreadsheet or a data base.
    2. Eliminate the request by bots, spiders or crawlers.
    3. Generate Equivalence Classes considering the attributes
    <HTTP Requested, URL Requested, Status Code>
    4. Filter the Equivalence Classes with values <GET,
    *.html, 200>, <GET, *.php, 200>,<GET, *.aspx, 200>,
    <GET, *.jsp, 200>, <GET, *php*, 200> and <GET, /, 200>
    5. All other Equivalence Classes are saved in another
    file for statistical analysis if required.
End
```

Algorithm 2.1 Generation of Equivalence Classes from Web logs for successful user requests

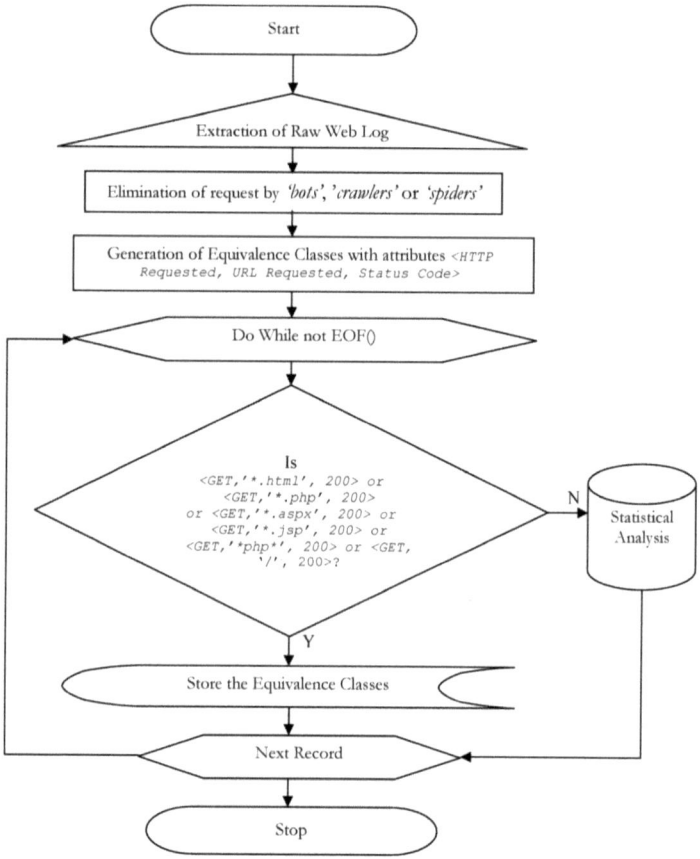

Fig. 2.1 Process Flow Diagram for generating Equivalence Classes from Web logs for successful user requests

Web Log - Notepad

File Edit Format View Help

```
b3091254.crawl.yahoo.net - - [01/Jan/2011:00:12:15 +051800] "GET /index.php?option=com_content&task=view&id=21&Itemid=23 HTTP/1.0" 20
m/help/us/ysearch/slurp)"b3090864.crawl.yahoo.net - - [01/Jan/2011:00:24:35 +051800] "GET / HTTP/1.0" 200 51357 "-" "Mozilla/5.0 (com
; MJ12bot/v1.3.3; http://www.majestic12.co.uk/bot.php?+)"5.ovz.chicago.123systems.net - - [01/Jan/2011:00:28:56 +051800] "GET /index.
ion=com_content&task=view HTTP/1.0" 200 41562 "-" "Mozilla/5.0 (compatible; MJ12bot/v1.3.3; http://www.majestic12.co.uk/bot.php?+)"5.
//www.majestic12.co.uk/bot.php?+)"5.ovz.chicago.123systems.net - - [01/Jan/2011:00:29:35 +051800] "GET /index.php?option=com_content&
] "GET /index.php?option=com_content&task=view&id=162&Itemid=94 HTTP/1.0" 200 41809 "-" "Mozilla/5.0 (compatible; MJ12bot/v1.3.3; htt
(compatible; MJ12bot/v1.3.3; http://www.majestic12.co.uk/bot.php?+)"5.ovz.chicago.123systems.net - - [01/Jan/2011:00:30:15 +051800] "
- [01/Jan/2011:00:30:29 +051800] "GET /index.php?option=com_content&task=view&id=6&Itemid=9 HTTP/1.0" 200 42782 "-" "Mozilla/5.0 (com
Windows NT 6.1; en-US) AppleWebKit/534.10 (KHTML, like Gecko) Chrome/8.0.552.224 Safari/534.10"117.196.136.242 - - [01/Jan/2011:00:46
ozilla/5.0 (Windows; U; Windows NT 6.1; en-US) AppleWebKit/534.10 (KHTML, like Gecko) Chrome/8.0.552.224 Safari/534.10"117.196.136.24
.1" 200 691 "http://www.nestgroup.net/" "Mozilla/5.0 (Windows; U; Windows NT 6.1; en-US) AppleWebKit/534.10 (KHTML, like Gecko) Chrom
_home/images/SFOlogo.jpg HTTP/1.1" 200 21766 "http://www.nestgroup.net/" "Mozilla/5.0 (Windows; U; Windows NT 6.1; en-US) AppleWebKit
6:11 +051800] "GET /images/stories/home/whtarro.gif HTTP/1.1" 200 61 "http://www.nestgroup.net/" "Mozilla/5.0 (Windows; U; Windows NT
Jan/2011:00:46:11 +051800] "GET /images/stories/home/index_05.gif HTTP/1.1" 200 964 "http://www.nestgroup.net/" "Mozilla/5.0 (Windows
Chrome/8.0.552.224 Safari/534.10"117.196.136.242 - - [01/Jan/2011:00:46:20 +051800] "GET /templates/sfo_about2/images/bg.gif HTTP/1.1
0:46:20 +051800] "GET /templates/sfo_about2/images/locations.jpg HTTP/1.1" 200 10450 "http://www.nestgroup.net/index.php?option=com_c
TP/1.1" 200 1731 "http://www.nestgroup.net/nestit/" "Mozilla/5.0 (Windows; U; Windows NT 6.1; en-US) AppleWebKit/534.10 (KHTML, like
i/534.10"219.64.67.45.hyd-cdma.dialup.vsnl.net.in - - [01/Jan/2011:00:55:05 +051800] "GET /nestit/images/nestit_04.png HTTP/1.1" 200
nestgroup.net/nestit/" "Mozilla/5.0 (Windows; U; Windows NT 6.1; en-US) AppleWebKit/534.10 (KHTML, like Gecko) Chrome/8.0.552.224 Saf
.dialup.vsnl.net.in - - [01/Jan/2011:00:55:08 +051800] "GET /nestit/images/nestit_10.png HTTP/1.1" 200 1434 "http://www.nestgroup.net
Windows NT 6.1; en-US) AppleWebKit/534.10 (KHTML, like Gecko) Chrome/8.0.552.224 Safari/534.10"219.64.67.45.hyd-cdma.dialup.vsnl.net.
GET /nestit/images/point.gif HTTP/1.1" 200 880 "http://www.nestgroup.net/nestit/" "Mozilla/5.0 (Windows; U; Windows NT 6.1; en-US) Ap
cko) Chrome/8.0.552.224 Safari/534.10"219.64.67.45.hyd-cdma.dialup.vsnl.net.in - - [01/Jan/2011:00:55:15 +051800] "GET /nestit/images
1389 "http://www.nestgroup.net/nestit/" "Mozilla/5.0 (Windows; U; Windows NT 6.1; en-US) AppleWebKit/534.10 (KHTML, like Gecko) Chrom
Jan/2011:01:05:02 +051800] "GET /nestit/images/nestit2_07.png HTTP/1.1" 200 2494 "http://www.nestgroup.net/nestit/" "Mozilla/5.0 (Win
dows NT 6.1; en-US) AppleWebKit/534.10 (KHTML, like Gecko) Chrome/8.0.552.224 Safari/534.10"219.64.67.45.hyd-cdma.dialup.vsnl.net.in
nl.net.in - - [01/Jan/2011:01:05:14 +051800] "GET /favicon.ico HTTP/1.1" 404 290 "-" "Mozilla/5.0 (Windows; U; Windows NT 6.1; en-US)
HTML, like Gecko) Chrome/8.0.552.224 Safari/534.10"219.64.67.45.hyd-cdma.dialup.vsnl.net.in - - [01/Jan/2011:01:12:04 +051800] "GET /
cdma.dialup.vsnl.net.in - - [01/Jan/2011:01:12:38 +051800] "GET /nestit/contact.html HTTP/1.1" 200 21599 "http://www.nestgroup.net/ne
```

Fig. 2.2 Input File for generation of Equivalence Classes for successful user requests

1	IP		User Authentication	Date & Time	HTTP	URL Requested	Protocol Version	Response Status	Bytes	Referrer URL	Browser and Version	Operating System and Version
2	117.196.136.242	-	-	1/1/2011 0:45	GET	/	HTTP/1.1	200	51357	http //www.nest	Mozilla/5.0	(Windows;
3	117.196.136.242	-	-	1/1/2011 0:46	GET	/index.php?optioncom_content&taskvi	HTTP/1.1	200	42511	http //www.nest	Mozilla/5.0	(Windows;
4	219.64.67.45.hyd	-	-	1/1/2011 0:55	GET	/nestit/	HTTP/1.1	200	17378	http //www.goog	Mozilla/5.0	(Windows;
5	219.64.67.45.hyd	-	-	1/1/2011 0:55	GET	/nestit/images/homebanner.swf	HTTP/1.1	200	99874	http //www.nest	Mozilla/5.0	(Windows;
6	219.64.67.45.hyd	-	-	1/1/2011 1:05	GET	/nestit/services.html	HTTP/1.1	200	9258	http //www.nest	Mozilla/5.0	(Windows;
7	219.64.67.45.hyd	-	-	1/1/2011 1:12	GET	/nestit/gis.html	HTTP/1.1	200	8249	http //www.nest	Mozilla/5.0	(Windows;
8	219.64.67.45.hyd	-	-	1/1/2011 1:12	GET	/nestit/contact.html	HTTP/1.1	200	21599	http //www.nest	Mozilla/5.0	(Windows;
9	host-196.218.41.	-	-	1/1/2011 1:16	GET	/	HTTP/1.1	200	51357	http //www.goog	Mozilla/4.0	(compatible;
10	115.113.10.228.s	-	-	1/1/2011 2:33	GET	/index.php?optioncom_content&taskvi	HTTP/1.1	200	46456	http //www.goog	Mozilla/4.0	(compatible;
11	91.201.66.28	-	-	1/1/2011 2:34	GET	/	HTTP/1.0	200	51357	http //autoschoo	Mozilla/4.0	(compatible;
12	173.193.5.181-st	-	-	1/1/2011 3:29	GET	//index.php?optioncom_user&viewrese	HTTP/1.1	200	42458	-	libwww-perl/5.837	
13	91.201.66.135	-	-	1/1/2011 3:33	GET	/	HTTP/1.0	200	51357	http //xn--c1ab0	Mozilla/4.0	(compatible;

FilteredLog / Bots / Request / Response / SupportFiles / Uncategorized Bots / Baiduspider / Bin

Fig. 2.3 Cleaned Web Log in Extended Log Format

2.1.3 User and Session Identification

A time out of 30 minutes is used to identify a user session in a Common Log Format. Each request from the same IP before 30 minutes is considered as the same user [[35]Srivastava00]. Since the log file used was an Extended Log File, the browser with its version and operating system with its version is also considered for identifying users and user sessions. Different values of the browser or operating system on the same client represent different users. Even if the IP address is the same, if there is a change in browser or operating system, it can be assumed that it is a different user [[37]Suresh06]. After user session identification, if the task to be performed is association rule mining or frequent itemset mining, the log file is further pre-processed to obtain records in the form $<T_{id}, p_1, p_2, ...p_n>$, where T_{id} represents the transaction id and $p_1, p_2,...p_n$ represents the pages requested. The data set 1 is a raw log file of a business organization NeST ranging from January 1, 2011 to March 31, 2011 and data set 2 is a raw log file of an academic institution BPC College ranging from November 1, 2012 to December 31, 2012. Table 2.2 shows the statistics of Web log data before and after pre-processing for data set 1 and Table 2.3 shows the statistics of Web log data before and after pre-processing for data set 2.

Table 2.2 Statistics of Web log data before and after pre-processing for data set 1

		January 1-31, 2011	February 1-28, 2011	March 1-31, 2011
1	Total number of records	286,867	275,871	305,860
2	Number of records after removing search engine visits	258,594	244,393	272,751
3	Number of records after pre-processing	20,934	19,238	20,434
4	Percentage in reduction	92.70%	93.03%	93.32%
5	Total number of users	8,677	7,908	8,430

Table 2.3 Statistics of Web log data before and after pre-processing for data set 2

		November 1-30, 2012	December 1-31, 2012
1	Total number of records	119,519	141,256
2	Number of records after removing search engine visits	113,909	134,626
3	Number of records after pre-processing	4,930	6,908
4	Percentage in reduction	95.87%	95.11%
5	Total number of users	1,721	1,989

2.1.4 Pre-fetching and Caching

If the mining of Web logs is performed for pre-fetching and caching of Web pages in proxy servers, then the pre-processing is done in a different way.

The Web objects like images, sounds, movies cannot be eliminated. References to embedded objects are usually preceded by their HTML container [98Yang01]. The container pages include pages with extension *.html, *.jsp, *.aspx, *.php etc. If the status code is successful, then the number of bytes transferred is important for caching and pre-fetching purposes. Algorithm 2.2 shows the generation of Equivalence Classes from Web logs for pre-fetching and caching purposes. Fig 2.4 shows the Process Flow Diagram for pre-processing of Web log files for pre-fetching and caching. Fig. 2.2 shows the input file for pre-processing of Web logs for pre-fetching and caching. The result of pre-processing for pre-fetching and caching is shown in Fig. 2.5.

Input: A raw Web log file in Extended Log Format.

Output: A file with URL requested (container pages), its frequency and total bytes transferred.

Method:
```
Begin
    1. Extract the fields from a raw log file to a
       spreadsheet or a data base.
    2. Eliminate the request by bots, spiders or crawlers.
    3. Generate    Equivalence   classes   considering   the
       attributes <HTTP Requested, URL Requested, Status
       Code>
    4. Filter the Equivalence Classes with values <GET, *.*,
       200> and <GET, /, 200>
    5. Compute the total bytes transferred including the
       embedded objects for each container page.
    6. Calculate the frequency of each container page.
    7. Eliminate all other fields excluding container page
       and total bytes transferred.
End
```

Algorithm 2.2 Generation of Equivalence Classes from Web logs for pre-fetching and caching

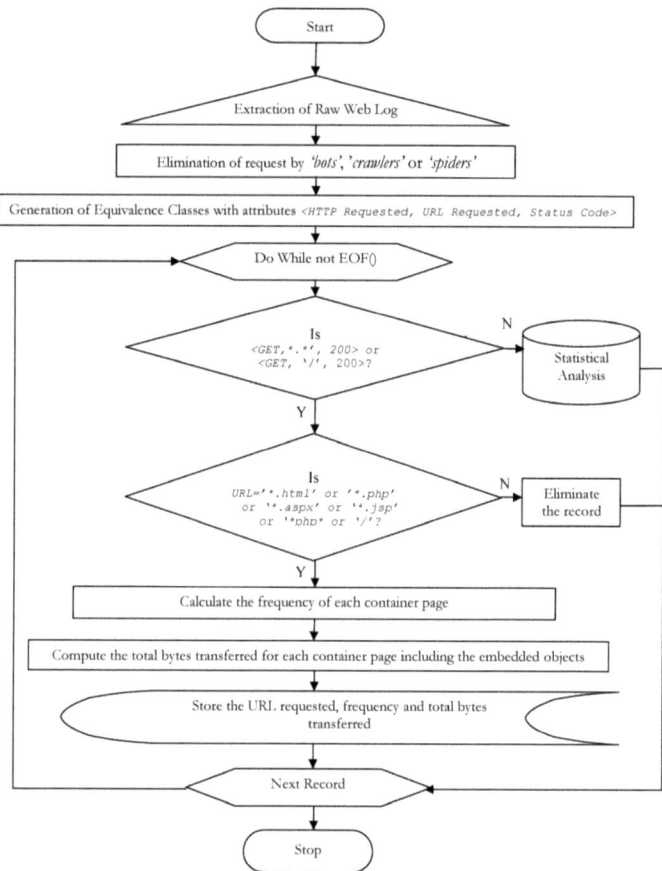

Fig. 2.4 Process Flow Diagram for pre-processing of Web logs for pre-fetching and caching

	URL requested	Frequency	Total Bytes
1			
2	/	313	200270
3	/index.php?option=com_content&task=view&id=101&Itemid=85	69	212084
4	/index.php?option=com_performs&formid=1&Itemid=115	69	145576
5	/index.php?option=com_content&task=view&id=70&Itemid=72	62	42511
6	/index.php?option=com_content&task=view&id=68&Itemid=70	52	40564
7	/index.php?option=com_frontpage&Itemid=1	47	51357
8	/index.php?option=com_content&task=view&id=3&Itemid=3	27	150661
9	/index.php?option=com_content&task=view&id=59&Itemid=61	25	402515
10	/index.php?option=com_content&task=blogcategory&id=103&It	22	124846
11	/index.php?option=com_content&task=view&id=2&Itemid=2	22	124286
12	/index.php?option=com_content&task=view&id=26&Itemid=97	22	554724
13	/index.php?option=com_content&task=view&id=72&Itemid=74	22	40796
14	/index.php?Itemid=85&id=101&option=com_content&task=view	21	244314
15	/index.php?option=com_joomap&Itemid=118	19	62382

Fig. 2.5 Results of pre-processing for pre-fetching and caching

2.2 Web Usage Analytics

The three main ways to access a Website are

1) A search engine request
2) A link from another Website (referring sites)
3) The Website root by typing the URL of the Website in a Web browser [100Ortega10].

There are differences in user behavior according to the entry point to a Website. [101Kohavi03] offers several recommendations that include analysis of human versus bot traffic, univariate data, session timeouts, form errors, micro-conversions, search, real estate usage, product affinities (associations), migrators and geographical data. Several of this advanced analysis is based on the construction of a customer signature, which in turn benefits from additional overlays, such as third-party demographic attributes. Usage analytics includes origin of visits, referring sites, most popular keywords used by the visitor to arrive at a Website, user agents including browser and operating system [235Jose12] [238;jose12]. Algorithm 2.3 gives

51

the pseudo code for extracting origin of visits, referring sites and keywords used to arrive at a Website. Input file for Algorithm 2.3 is a pre-processed Web log file obtained from the output of Algorithm 2.1. Fig. 2.6 depicts the Process Flow Diagram for extracting origin of visits, referrer pages and keywords used to arrive at a Website.

Input: A pre-processed Web log file in Extended Log Format
Output: A file containing origin of visits, referrer pages and keywords
Method:

```
Begin
  Open pre-processed Web_log
  Set   directEntry=0,   keywordList=NULL,   referrerList=NULL,
  keywordPattern= {"?q","&q","#q"}
  Do While not EOF()
  URL = getreferrerURL(Web_log)
    If URL = "-" then
     increment directEntry
    EndIf
    If substring(URL,keywordPattern) then
     keyword = findKeyword(URL)
        If keyword is NEW then
           Add keyword to keywordList
           Set keywordList(keyword).count = 1
        Else
           increment keywordList(keyword).count
        EndIf
    EndIf
    If URL is NEW then
     Add URL to referrerList
     Set referrerList(URL).count = 1
    Else
     increment referrerList(URL).count
```

```
    EndIf
  EndDo
  Close Web_log
End
```

Algorithm 2.3 Pseudo code for extracting origin of visits, referring sites and keywords used to arrive at a Website

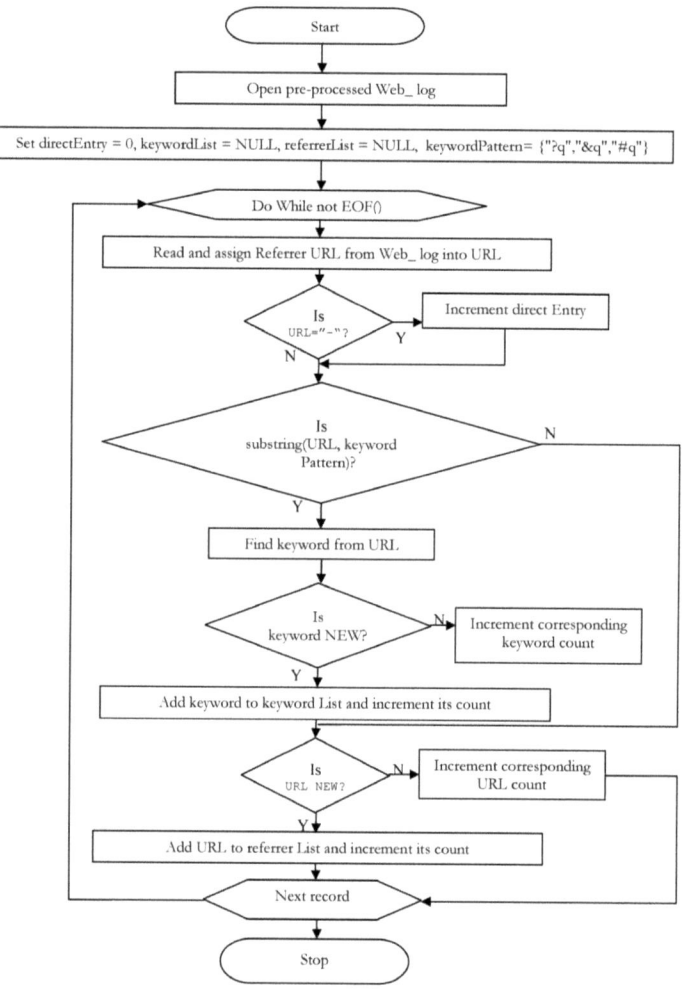

Fig. 2.6 Process Flow Diagram for extracting origin of visits, referrer pages and keywords used to arrive at a Website

2.2.1 Origin of Visits and Referring Sites

Origin of visits means the different ways to access a Website. Fig. 2.7 shows graphical representation of the origin of visits and the percentage for data set 1 and Fig. 2.8 shows the graphical representation of the origin of visits and the percentage for data set 2. The graphical representation revealed that majority of users arrived at Website 1 using search engine Google (59%). 23.09% of the users used direct URL address to arrive at this Website and 16.55% arrived by referring from other Websites. A small proportion of users arrived at this Website from Yahoo (0.7%) and Bing (0.66%).

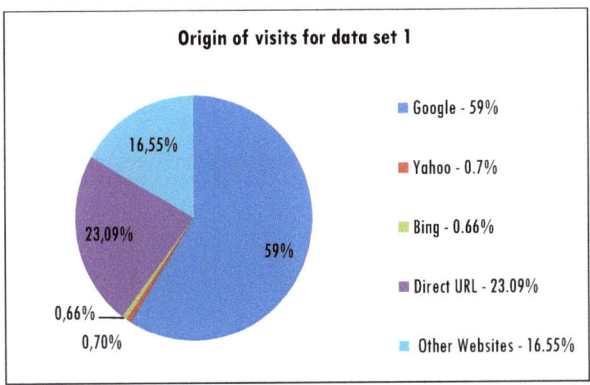

Fig. 2.7 Origin of visits and the percentage for data set 1

In the case of Website 2, the graphical representation shows that majority of the visitors arrived at this site by using the direct URL address in a browser (54.28%). The users who used direct URL can be considered as familiar users of this site or people who know the Website address of this organization. This is followed by users arrived from Google (41.9%).Other users happened to arrive at Website 2 from other linking Websites or referring sites (2.54%), Yahoo (0.51%) and Bing (0.77%).

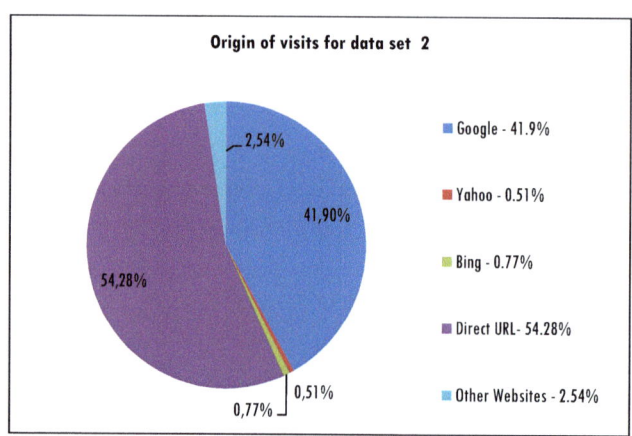

Fig. 2.8 Origin of visits and the percentage for data set 2

Table 2.4 shows the percentage of users from top referring sites for data set 1 and Table 2.5 shows the percentage of users from top referring sites for data set 2.

Table 2.4 Percentage of users from top referring sites for data set 1

Referring site	Percentage of users
www.nestsoftware.com	24.50%
www.linkedin.com	13.20%
www.opterna.com	12.90%
www.keralaindex.com	12.60%
en.wikipedia.org	11.50%
others	25.30%

Table 2.5 Percentage of users from top referring sites for data set 2

Referring site	Percentage of users
bpccollege.libsoft.org	42.21%
www.bpcconferences.in	23.80%
en.wikipedia.org	6.21%
www.sitefinder.co.in	2.50%
search.mywebsearch.com	1.32%
others	23.96%

2.2.2 Keywords

The referrer field is further extracted to identify popular search keywords used. It is helpful in identifying the most preferred content by the Web user. There are several keywords used by visitors to access the Website. Search engines analyzing query log data and showing several models about how users search and how users use search engine results are studied by [[102]Baeza-Yates05]. Keyword analysis allows identifying properties over the keyword collections that frequently are considered to make queries. The frequently used keywords play a vital role in identifying the search keywords used by various users. The referrer field contains substrings which lead to identify the popular keywords used. These results are helpful in redesigning the Websites, search engine optimization and stuffing of meta-tags. Table 2.6 shows the most frequent keywords used to access Website 1 and Table 2.7 shows the most frequent keywords used to access Website 2 by different users. Among the visitors through search engines, the keyword *sfo technologies* was the most frequently used keyword in data set 1 and *bpc college* was the most frequently used keyword in data set 2. In addition to the keywords mentioned in Table 2.6 and Table 2.7, there are several other keywords whose percentage is very less. Hence these keywords are not considered relevant.

Table 2.6 Frequent keywords used to access Website 1

Keywords	Percentage
sfo technologies	41.33%
nest group	17.97%
network systems	10.87%
nest power electronics	10.38%
nest photonics	7.38%
nest group Trivandrum	5.32%
nest information technology	4.75%
others	2.00%

Table 2.7 Frequent keywords used to access Website 2

Keywords	Percentage
bpc college	55.80%
bpc college piravom	19.14%
www.bpc.ac.in	9.60%
baselios poulose ii catholicos college	8.25%
piravom	3.20%
placement bpccollege	1.30%
others	2.71%

2.2.3 User Agents

The user agents are analyzed to understand the browser and operating system used. This is done to understand popular browsers with its version used by visitors to arrive at a Website. This study is useful in analyzing the user's preference of browsers. Similarly the operating system with its version used by visitors is also recorded in the log file. This gives a detailed account of the various operating systems with its version used by visitors. Algorithm 2.4 gives the pseudo code for extracting browsers and operating systems. Fig. 2.9 illustrates the Process Flow Diagram for extracting browsers and operating system. Table 2.8 shows the statistics of different browsers with its version used by visitors in data set 1 and Table 2.9 shows the statistics of different browsers with its version used by visitors in data set 2. Table 2.10 gives the statistics of various operating systems with its versions found in data set 1 and Table 2.11 gives the statistics of various operating systems with its versions found in data set 2.

Input: A pre-processed Web log file
Output: Browsers and Operating systems
Method:
```
Begin
   Open pre-processed Web_log
   Set browserList = NULL, osList = NULL
   Do While not EOF()
    useragent = getuserAgentString(Web_log)
    browser = parseBrowser(useragent)
    os = parseOS(useragent)
        If browser is NEW then
           Add browser to browserList
           Set browserList(browser).count = 1
        Else
           increment browserList(browser).count
        EndIf
        If os is NEW then
           Add os to osList
           Set osList(os).count = 1
        Else
           increment osList(os).count
        EndIf
   EndDo
   Close Web_log
 End
```

Algorithm 2.4 Pseudo code for extracting browsers and operating systems

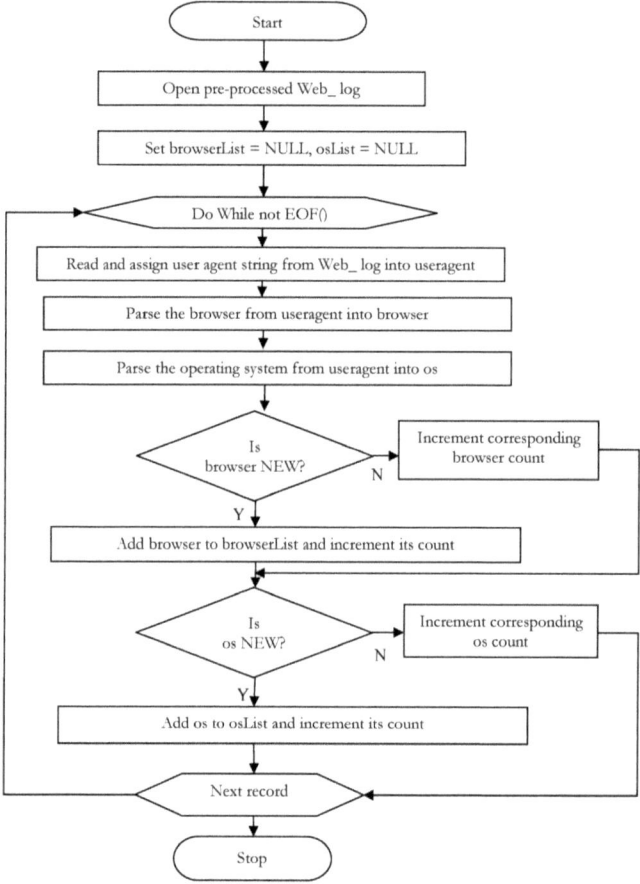

Fig. 2.9 Process Flow Diagram for extracting browsers and operating system

Table 2.8 Statistics of different browsers and its version used by visitors in data set 1

Browser	Percentage
Google Chrome	50.91%
Firefox Mozilla Version 5.0	20.94%
Microsoft Internet Explorer Version 8.0	14.15%
Microsoft Internet Explorer Version 6.0	10.78%
Microsoft Internet Explorer Version 7.0	0.21%
Opera Version 9.8	0.19%
Microsoft Internet Explorer Version 9.0	0.06%
BlackBerry	0.06%
Microsoft Internet Explorer Version 4.01	0.06%
Microsoft Internet Explorer Version 5.5	0.04%
Microsoft Internet Explorer Version 5.0	0.04%
Others	2.56%

Table 2.9 Statistics of different browsers and its version used by visitors in data set 2

Browser	Percentage
Google Chrome	33.30%
Microsoft Internet Explorer Version 8.0	22.20%
Microsoft Internet Explorer Version 6.0	6.13%
Firefox Mozilla Version 18.0	5.66%
Microsoft Internet Explorer Version 7.0	4.20%
Microsoft Internet Explorer Version 6.0	3.42%
Firefox Mozilla Version 17.0	3.21%
Microsoft Internet Explorer Version 7.0	2.06%
Firefox Mozilla Version 12.0	1.88%
Firefox Mozilla Version 11.0	1.16%
Opera Version 7.0	0.93%
Others	15.85%

Table 2.10 Statistics of various operating systems and its version found in data set 1

Operating System	Percentage
Windows XP	60.28%
Windows NT 7	25.30%
Windows Vista	9.15%
Windows XP Professional x64	2.75%
Windows 2000	0.33%
Debian-3.0.6-1	0.13%
Ubuntu 10.10	0.23%
Ubuntu-feisty	0.10%
Linux x86_64	0.13%
Linux i686 (x86_64)	0.10%
Linux i686	1.26%
Ubuntu 10.04	0.07%
Ubuntu 9.10	0.04%
Ubuntu dapper-security	0.13%

Table 2.11 Statistics of various operating systems and its version found in data set 2

Operating System	Percentage
Windows 7	40%
Windows XP	35.80%
Windows XP Professional x64	16.85%
Linux x86_64	3.44%
Windows Vista	1.36%
Windows 8	1.15%
Ubuntu	0.49%
Ubuntu 10.04	0.37%
Ubuntu 12.04	0.27%
Ubuntu 10.10	0.16%
Windows 2000	0.06%
Ubuntu 9.04	0.04%
Windows NT 4.0	0.01%

2.3 Conclusion

Rough set theory and indiscernibility relation has found applications in many domains like engineering, environment, banking, medicine and others. This Chapter is an attempt to highlight another application of indiscernibility relation in rough set theory, which is the pre-processing of Web log files. Pre-processing of Web log files is the very first step in Web Usage Mining. The advantage of this method of pre-processing is the generation of different Equivalence Classes which can be further used for statistical analysis including prediction. The pre-processed file can be used for various Web Usage Mining task functionalities.

The Extended Log File is an immense source of information to identify user behavior as well as origin of user visits. It is important to know the origin of visitors for a Website developer so that a better search engine optimization can be performed. Understanding frequent keywords used by a visitor to arrive at a Website is important while creating meta-tags. Search engines like Google uses several criteria for determining the PageRank. These keywords could be included as heading in a Web page or appear in bold font which may increase the PageRank. Thus the Website may appear closer to the search results. The Websites referring to a particular Website provides information about the different types of Websites providing link to one's Website. The information about the browser with its version is essential because Website designers may develop Websites that require viewing capabilities which may not be supported by certain browsers. The user agent field gives information about the new browsers and operating systems used as well as the outdated browsers and operating systems used by visitors to access the Website.

2.4 Publications based on this Chapter

[1] Jeeva Jose, P. Sojan Lal, "An Indiscernibility Approach for Pre-processing of Web Log Files", International Journal of Internet Computing, vol. 1, no. 3, 2012, pp.58-61. ISSN: 2231-6965

[2] Jeeva Jose, P. Sojan Lal, "Extracting Extended Web Logs to Identify the Origin of Visits and Search Keywords", Intelligent Informatics, Advances in Intelligent Systems and Computing, Springer, vol. 182, 2012, pp. 435-441. DOI: 10.1007/978-3-642-32063-7_46

[3] Jeeva Jose, P. Sojan Lal, "Extracting Extended Web Logs to Identify the Origin of Visits and Search Keywords", Proceedings of the International Symposium on Intelligent Informatics, organized by RMK Engineering College, Chennai, August 4-5, 2012. pp. 435-441. ISBN: 978-3-642-32062-0[Selected for publication in Intelligent Informatics, Springer (Publication 2)].

[4] Jeeva Jose, P. Sojan Lal, "An Indiscernibility Approach for Pre-processing of Web Log Files", Proceedings of the International Conference on Electrical Engineering and Computer Science, IRNet, Trivandrum, May 12, 2012, pp.39-43. ISBN: 978-93-81693-58-2 [Selected for publication in International Journal of Internet Computing (Publication 1)].

>> *End of Chapter 2* <<

Chapter 3: Clustering of Users and User Sessions

An important research topic in Web Usage Mining is the clustering of Web users and Web user sessions based on their common properties. Clustering Web sessions is the problem of grouping Web sessions based on similarity and maximizing the intra-group similarity while minimizing the inter-group similarity. Clustering of users tend to establish groups of users exhibiting similar browsing patterns. Such knowledge is especially useful for inferring user demographics in order to perform market segmentation in E-commerce applications or provide personalized Web content to users. The knowledge acquired from Web user session clusters have enormous applications like pre-fetching pages between clients and the proxies, creating adaptive Websites etc. In this work, the clusters of users and similar user sessions are generated based on the Entry Pages to a Website.

3.1 Background Literature

There are several works in literature that had studied about user traffic and clustering of user sessions. [^{104}Cooley97] has suggested different ways of identifying a user from a Web log. It also differentiates user sessions from transactions and suggested ways for path analysis to determine the most frequently visited paths in a Website. A review of various methods and algorithms for data clustering was done by [^{105}Jain99] which can also be applied to Web log data. The access patterns of Web users can be extracted and organized into sessions which represent episodes between the Web client and the Web server. Using attribute oriented induction, the sessions are then generalized based on page hierarchy and these generalized sessions are clustered using hierarchical method of clustering in [^{106}Fu99].

A multilevel scheme for clustering large number of Web users from their past access behavior is proposed by [^{107}Xiao01]. Clustering of navigation patterns based on sequence alignment method which captures sequential relationship in data and extract sequences with similar behavior patterns not only with regard to content but also the order of pages that are visited in a sequence is done by [108]Hay99]. A principled approach to identify user sessions based on two sources of evidence time interval and search pattern obtained from analyzing a large batch of Web search logs to facilitate the usage of contexts behind Web user's searches is done in [109]He02]. A new method for measuring similarities between Web sessions that takes into account the sequence of event in a click-stream visitation and similarities between pages visited in a session is introduced in [110]Wang02].

[111]Piramuthu03] has used machine learning methods specifically decision trees to analyze Web traffic. [112]Xing04] has proposed a new concept, *preference*, which represents user navigation interest and intention accurately by selection and viewing time situation. [114]Wang05] has proposed a concurrent neuro-fuzzy model to discover and analyze useful knowledge from Web log data and made use of the cluster information generated by a self organizing map for pattern analysis and a fuzzy inference system to capture the chaotic trend to provide short-term (hourly) and long-term (daily) Web traffic trend predictions.

A hierarchical clustering algorithm to generate Web sessions further processed by centroid and BLEM2 classifiers is proposed by [115] Khasawneh05]. GHIC: A Hierarchical Pattern-Based Clustering Algorithm for grouping Web transactions that groups customer transactions such that itemsets generated from each cluster, while similar to each other, are different from generated by others is proposed by [116]Yang05].[117]Hong-fang06] has used a technique of mining user traversed sub-paths and these are finally merged to identify user preferred paths.[118]Song06] has discovered both the user clusters and Web page clusters by vector analysis and fuzzy set theory based methods. The frequent access paths are recognized based on Web page clusters and take into account the underlying structure of a Website. This method does not require identification of user sessions from Web server logs. Both a user and a page can be assigned to more than one cluster.

[119Tripathy07] proposes a rough set approach for clustering of Web data for knowledge discovery in World Wide Web for E-business. A work on study of user sessions which have been reconstructed by means of heuristic methods was done by [120Agosti07]. Since no personal data are available to track each user, the heuristics used to identify users and sessions suggested that authentication would be required as it would allow Web servers to identify users, track their requests and more importantly create profiles to tailor specific needs. Moreover, authentication would also help to solve the problem concerning crawler accesses, granting access to some sections of the Website only to registered users and blocking crawlers using faked user agents. [121Chaofeng07] introduced a new method for measuring similarities between Web sessions that takes into account not only the URL but also the viewing time of the visited Web page.

A new indiscernibility based rough agglomerative hierarchical clustering algorithm for sequential data is introduced by [122Kumar07]. The rough clusters resulting from the above mentioned algorithm provide interpretations of different navigation orientations of users present in the sessions. Though there are several works for clustering Web user sessions, the problem of assessing the quality of user session clusters in order to make inferences regarding the user's navigation behavior was done by [123Pallis07]. [124Alam08] has proposed a particle swarm intelligence based algorithm for clustering Web users. A general sequence based clustering method by using new sequence representation schemes in association with Markov models is proposed by [125Park08].

A novel approach for clustering Web user sessions using rough set theory is proposed by [127Jyoti09]. [128Chen09] address the problem in existing Web user clustering by clustering Web users based on the evolution of Web usage data. In this a set of Web users and their associated historical Web usage data will be given. From this how their usage data change over time and mine evolutionary patterns from each user's usage history is studied. The discovered patterns capture the characteristics of changes to a Web user's information needs. Web user clusters generated in this way provide novel and useful knowledge for various personalized Web applications, including Web advertisement and Web caching. [129Yang10] has proposed a simple and powerful approach to profile user's Web browsing behavior for the purpose of user identification. [131Zhu10] has proposed a new algorithm based on average time threshold value for Web user sessions. By adjusting the time threshold value individually, compared to the traditional algorithm that defines a uniform threshold value for all user's Web pages, this algorithm can identify the long session more accurately.

[132Xinhua11] has proposed a session identification algorithm based on dynamic timeout. [133Suresh11] has introduced an improved fuzzy c-means algorithm for clustering Web user sessions. [134Vijayalakshmi11] has proposed an algorithm which systematically explores a pattern-growth approach for efficient mining of sequential patterns in large sequence database. This approach adopts a (divide and conquer) pattern growth in which sequence databases are recursively projected into a set of smaller projected databases based on current sequential pattern(s), and sequential patterns are grown in each projected databases by exploring only locally frequent fragments.

[135Hao11] has proposed a new approach for interleaved server session from Web server logs using m-order Markov model combined with a competitive algorithm. The proposed approach has the ability to reconstruct interleaved sessions from server logs. In [138Liu11], an improved Ward's method is proposed for Web user clustering. The only work that has shown the point of access (*Entry Page*) is in [100Ortega10]. Nevertheless there are no works in literature which investigate the behavior of user sessions from the entry point to a Website.

3.2 Deep Linking

It is important to analyze how a Website is being used. Usage information leads to better design of Websites and thereby enhancing the corporate objective of the organization. It is not mandatory that all visitors should enter into a Website through the Home page. A large number of visitors bypasses the Home page and enters into the Website through other pages (inner pages) in a Website. This is known as deep linking [[103]Spinello00]. From a Website owner's perspective, there are issues with deep linking as listed below [[68]Jose10].

- Home page is the prime page that explains the nature of the Website and offer hyperlinks to inner pages. When the Home page is bypassed, the intended method of navigation is defeated and the user may not access the prime information or may take longer time for navigation.
- Many organizations fix advertisement rates based on number of hits on the Home page. The deep linked entry will reduce the traffic to the Home page and thereby the advertising revenue that could be generated will be reduced.

3.3 Algorithm for Clustering Users based on *Entry Pages*

The mandatory pre-processing tasks mentioned in section 1.4 and 2.1 are performed before the clustering of users and the data set is reduced to less than 10%. Fig. 3.1 depicts the process of clustering users based on *Entry Pages*. The objective of clustering users based on *Entry Pages* is to see whether more number of users enter into a Website through Home page or other pages, the temporal information about the *Entry Pages*, the percentage of traffic through *Top Ten Entry Pages* etc [[241]Jose12]. Algorithm 3.1 shows clustering of users based on

Entry Pages to analyze deep linked traffic at a Website and Fig. 3.2 illustrates the Process Flow Diagram for clustering of users based on *Entry Pages*.

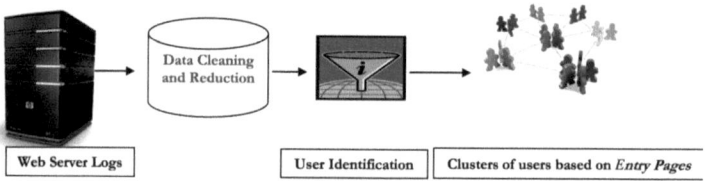

Fig. 3.1 Process of clustering users based on *Entry Pages*

Input: A pre-processed log file U with user names or IPs and path traversed.
Output: N clusters of users $\{C_1, C_2, \ldots C_n\}$ based on *Entry Pages*, where N represents the number of pages in a Website to which users have made their entry.
Method
```
Begin
    1. Initially assume all the users belong to one single
       cluster C, set Count_i to zero.
    2. Assign the first user with an Entry Page to cluster C_0,
       Count_0 = Count_0 + 1;
    3. When the next user comes assign to a cluster C_i with
       similar Entry Page, Count_i = Count_i+1
    4. If no cluster with similar Entry Pages exists, assign
       the user to a new cluster C_k(i≠k), Count_k = Count_k+1
    5. Repeat steps 4 and 5 until C is empty.
End
```

Algorithm 3.1 Clustering of users based on *Entry Pages*

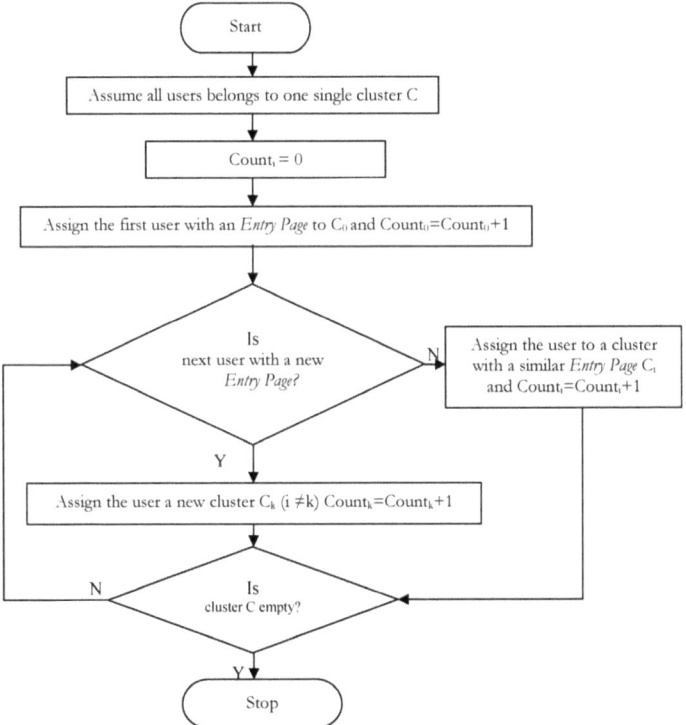

Fig. 3.2 Process Flow Diagram for clustering users based on *Entry Pages*

3.4 Results of Clustering Users based on *Entry Pages*

The algorithm is tested on two pre-processed Web log files. The first data set is of a business organization NeST ranging from January 1, 2011 to March 31, 2011 and the second data set is of an academic institution BPC College, ranging from November 1, 2012 to December 31, 2012. The results in Table 3.1 revealed that the number of clusters *(Entry Pages)* is not the same for all the three months for data set 1 and results in Table 3.2 revealed that the number of clusters (*Entry Pages*) is not the same for the two months in data set 2.

Table 3.1 Number of clusters (*Entry Pages*) for data set 1

Month	Number of clusters (***Entry Pages***)
January 1-31, 2011	277
February 1-28, 2011	269
March 1-31, 2011	260

Table 3.2 Number of clusters (*Entry Pages*) for data set 2

Month	Number of clusters (***Entry Pages***)
November 1-30, 2012	53
December 1-31, 2012	50

The *Top Ten Entry Pages* and the percentage of traffic for data set 1 and data set 2 is studied and the results are shown in Table 3.3 and Table 3.4 respectively. It revealed that the *Top Ten Entry Pages* are the same for all the three months for data set 1 and the *Top Ten Entry Pages* are the same for all the two months for data set 2.

Table 3.3 *Top Ten Entry Pages* and the percentage of traffic for data set 1

	Top Ten Entry Pages	Month					
		January 1-31, 2011	%	February 1-28, 2011	%	March 1-31, 2011	%
1	Home page	3806	43.86	3007	38.02	3342	39.64
2	/index.php?option=com_content&task=view&id=101&Itemid=85	447	5.15	372	4.70	455	5.40
3	/index.php?option=com_content&task=view&id=70&Itemid=72	407	4.69	388	4.91	393	4.66
4	/index.php?option=com_content&task=view&id=68&Itemid=70	340	3.92	297	3.76	390	4.63
5	/index.php?option=com_performs&formid=1&Itemid=115	301	3.47	353	4.46	305	3.62
6	/index.php?Itemid=85&id=101&option=com_content&task=view	187	2.16	253	3.20	270	3.20
7	/index.php?option=com_content&task=view&id=72&Itemid=74	175	2.02	142	1.80	158	1.87
8	/index.php?option=com_content&task=view&id=59&Itemid=61	174	2.01	140	1.77	152	1.80
9	/index.php?option=com_frontpage&Itemid=1	157	1.81	179	2.26	139	1.65
10	/index.php?option=com_content&task=view&id=2&Itemid=2	135	1.56	122	1.54	116	1.38

Table 3.4 *Top Ten Entry Pages* and the percentage of traffic for data set 2

	Top Ten Entry Pages	Month			
		November 1-30, 2012	%	December 1-31, 2012	%
1	Home page	741	43.06	833	41.88
2	/index.php	145	8.43	160	8.04
3	/principal.php	56	3.25	73	3.67
4	/photo_gallery.php	54	3.14	59	2.97
5	/contactus.php	19	1.10	25	1.26
6	/newscontent_arc.php	17	0.99	30	1.51
7	/ragging_prohibition.php	17	0.99	18	0.90
8	/clubs_vings.php	15	0.87	10	0.50
9	/excellence.php	12	0.70	13	0.65
10	/profile.php	10	0.58	14	0.70

Fig. 3.3 shows the percentage of visitors entered through Home page and other pages for data set 1 and Fig. 3.4 shows the percentage of visitors entered through Home page and other pages for data set 2. The percentage of traffic through Home page is 43.86% for January, 38.02% for February and 39.64% for the month of March in data set 1. The traffic through other pages contributed to 56.14% for January, 61.98% for February and 60.36% for March in data set 1. Similarly the percentage of traffic through Home page is 43.06% for November and 41.88% for December in data set 2. The traffic through other pages contributed to 56.94% for November and 58.12% for December in data set 2. It is observed that for all the three months in data set 1 and for all the two months in data set 2, the *Top Ten Entry Pages* are the same.

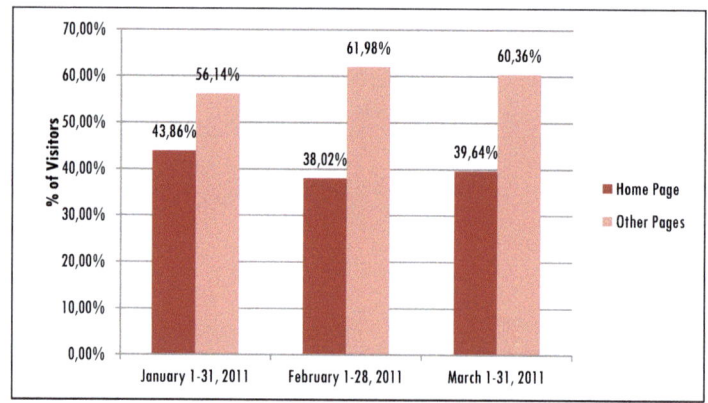

Fig. 3.3 Percentage of visitors entered through Home page and other pages for data set 1

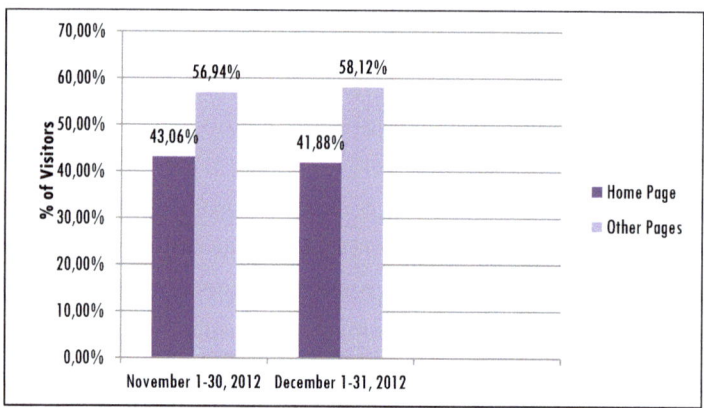

Fig. 3.4 Percentage of visitors entered through Home page and other pages for data set 2

Fig. 3.5 shows the comparison of the traffic through *Top Entry Pages* excluding Home page for data set 1 and Fig. 3.6 shows the comparison of the traffic through *Top Entry Pages* excluding Home page for data set 2.

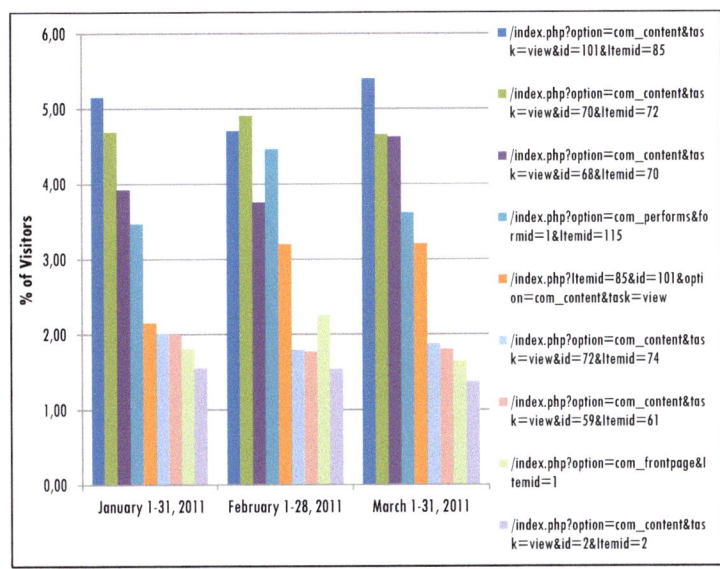

Fig. 3.5 Percentage of Traffic through *Top Entry Pages* excluding Home page for data set 1

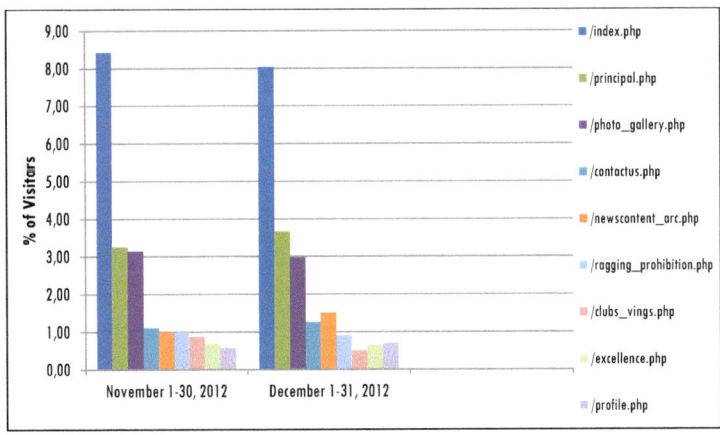

Fig. 3.6 Percentage of Traffic through *Top Entry Pages* excluding Home page for data set 2

3.5 Algorithm for Clustering User Sessions based on *Entry Pages*

The first data set is the Web log data of a business organization, NeST of one month ranging from March 1-31, 2011 and second data set is the Web log data of an academic institution BPC College of one month ranging from December 1-31, 2012. The mandatory pre-processing steps are done and user sessions are identified. The user sessions are again refined to remove sessions with one or two pages. This is because user may enter into the Website and leaves after one or two steps. These visits do not produce significant knowledge about Website usage. Similarly *Entry Pages* with count less than three is also removed. Table 3.5 shows the statistics of *Entry Pages* and user sessions for data set 1 and data set 2.

Table 3.5 Statistics of *Entry Pages* and user sessions for data set 1 and data set 2

	Data set 1 March 1-31, 2011	Data set 2 December 1-31, 2012
Total no: of user sessions	2558	950
No: of *Entry Pages*	300	50
No: of user sessions after removing sessions with <=2 pages	1989	381
No. of *Entry Pages* after removing count <=3	156	28

The methodology used for identifying similar user sessions is Rank Order Clustering algorithm for groupings based on attributes. This was developed by J. R King in 1980 for the formation of machine component cells in group technology [136Paneerselvam04]. The algorithm is used to obtain groupings of the user sessions based on pages visited. Suppose that for a given Website, there are m sessions $S=\{S_1, S_2, \ldots S_m\}$ accessing n different Web pages $P=\{P_1, P_2 \ldots P_n\}$. With the pages visited, a user-page incidence matrix is developed. The rows of the matrix represent user sessions and column of the matrix represents the pages visited. Consider this matrix as [Cij]. It contains 0 and 1 as entries. If the user i has visited page j, then the respective matrix element Cij is assumed as 1; otherwise it is assumed as 0. Figure 3.7 shows a user session-page incidence matrix.

The rank of each row or column is computed. Each column or row is assigned a weight W_0, W_1, …Wn. Each element is multiplied with the corresponding weight and sum of each row is calculated. The row with the highest value is considered to have the highest rank among the rows. The rows are interchanged in the descending order of their ranks. Similarly the column sum is computed and the column with the largest value is considered to have the highest rank among the columns. The columns are then interchanged in the descending order of their ranks. This process is repeated until all the ranks of rows and columns are in the increasing order of their ranks [237Jose12]. After final iteration the user session-page incidence matrix will appear as in Fig. 3.9. Algorithm 3.2 shows the Rank Order Clustering of user sessions and Fig 3.8 show the Process Flow Diagram for Rank Order Clustering of user sessions.

Input : A pre-processed log file U with user sessions.

Output : A user session – page incidence matrix in the descending order of ranks.

Method
```
Begin
    1. Construct the user session - page incidence matrix for
       user sessions with similar Entry Page.
    2. Assign the weights to each column and row.
    3. Repeat
    4. Compute the rank of all the rows
    5. Rearrange the rows of the matrix in descending order of
       their ranks
```

```
6. Compute the rank of all the columns
7. Rearrange the columns of the matrix in descending order
   of their ranks until there is no change.
End
```

Algorithm 3.2 Rank Order Clustering of user sessions

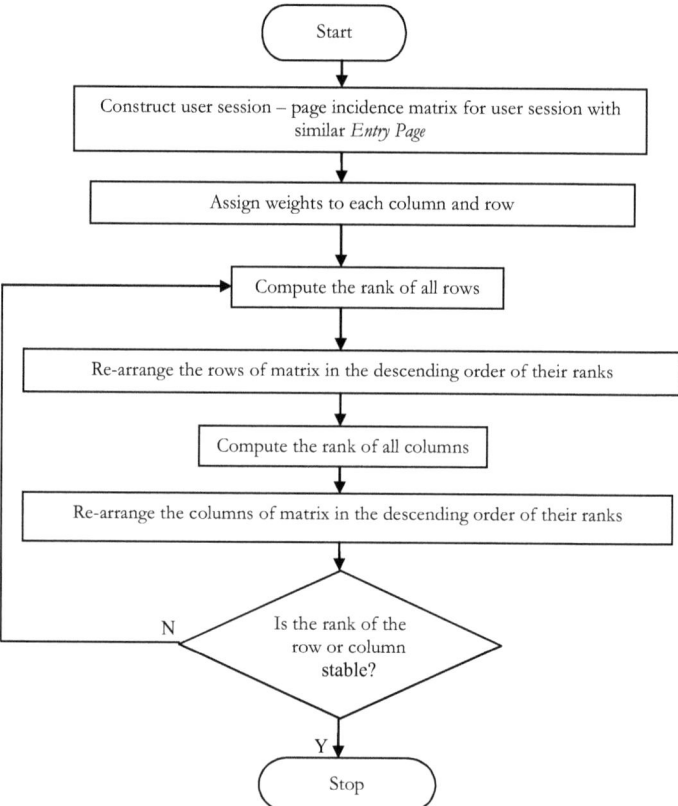

Fig. 3.8 Process Flow Diagram for Rank Order Clustering of user sessions

	pages visited (j)			
user session (i)	1	2	3	4
1	1	0	0	1
2	1	1	1	0
3	1	0	1	0
4	1	1	0	0
5	0	0	1	0

	pages visited (j)			
user session (i)	1	1	1	0
	1	1	0	0
	1	0	1	0
	1	0	0	1
	0	0	1	0

Fig. 3.7 User session-page incidence matrix   **Fig. 3.9** Results of final iteration

3.6 Results of Clustering User Sessions based on *Entry Pages*

Algorithm 3.2 is repeated for all user sessions with similar *Entry Page*. The aim is to find out whether all user sessions with similar *Entry Page* has similar behavior. The *Top Ten Entry Pages* and the user sessions are further analyzed. The graphical representation for *Top Ten Entry Pages*, the similar and dissimilar user sessions for data set 1 and data set 2 is given in Fig. 3.10 and Fig. 3.11 respectively. Table 3.6 and Table 3.7 shows the *Top Ten Entry Pages*, the total and similar user sessions for data set 1 and data set 2 respectively obtained as output of Algorithm 3.2. All other user sessions with various *Entry Pages* are not analyzed because the number of user sessions with those *Entry Pages* is very low.

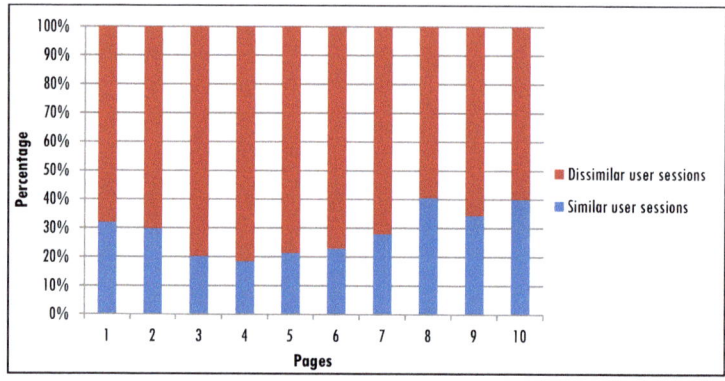

Fig. 3.10 Graphical representation of *Top Ten Entry Pages*, the similar and dissimilar user sessions for data set 1

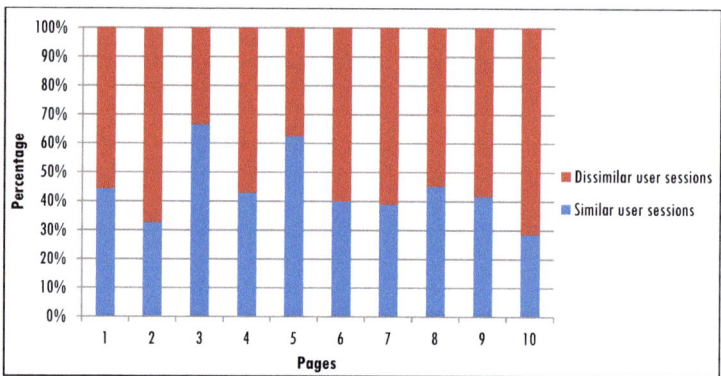

Fig. 3.11 Graphical representation of *Top Ten Entry Pages*, the similar and dissimilar user sessions for data set 2

The clustering results showed that for each *Entry Page* the percentage of similar user sessions varies between 18.48% and 40.54% in data set 1 and the percentage of similar user sessions varies between 28.57% and 66.67% in data set 2. User sessions showed more similarity in data set 2 as compared to data set 1.

Table 3.6 *Top Ten Entry Pages*, the total and similar user sessions for data set 1

	Top Ten Entry Pages	No: of user sessions	No: of similar user sessions	%
1	Home page	1309	418	31.93
2	/index.php?Itemid=85&id=101&option=com_content&task=view	97	29	29.90
3	/index.php?option=com_content&task=view&id=68&Itemid=70	94	19	20.21
4	/index.php?option=com_performs&formid=1&Itemid=115	92	17	18.48
5	/index.php?option=com_content&task=view&id=70&Itemid=72	75	16	21.33
6	/index.php?option=com_content&task=view&id=101&Itemid=85	61	14	22.95
7	/index.php?option=com_content&task=view&id=2&Itemid=2	43	12	27.91
8	/index.php?option=com_content&task=view&id=72&Itemid=74	37	15	40.54
9	/index.php?option=com_frontpage&Itemid=1	32	11	34.38
10	/index.php?option=com_content&task=view&id=59&Itemid=61	30	12	40.00

Table 3.7 *Top Ten Entry Pages*, the total and similar user sessions for data set 2

	Top Ten Entry Pages	No: of user sessions	No: of similar user sessions	%
1	Home page	559	248	44.36
2	/index.php	55	18	32.73
3	/principal.php	18	12	66.67
4	/photo_gallery.php	35	15	42.86
5	/contactus.php	16	10	62.50
6	/newscontent_arc.php	30	12	40.00
7	/ragging_prohibition.php	18	7	38.89
8	/clubs_vings.php	42	19	45.24
9	/excellence.php	12	5	41.67
10	/profile.php	14	4	28.57

3.7 Conclusion

In the proposed algorithm for clustering users based on *Entry Pages*, the number of clusters N varies from Website to Website depending on the entry of visitors to various pages. Unlike traditional K-means algorithm, the number of clusters need not be given as input. The clusters of users can be analyzed to study the deep linked entry from a particular demographic. The commercial organization's policy of fixing the advertisement rates based on the number of hits on the Home page needs to be reconsidered. The organization can think of search engine optimization to increase the number of users entering through Home pages. Otherwise the intended method of navigation is defeated. It is observed that the *Top Ten Entry Pages* in both data sets do not vary with time. The relation between *Entry Page* and time spent can also be analyzed to identify potential users.

The sessions are identified by grouping consecutive pages requested by the same user. The knowledge obtained is useful in many applications like dynamic hypertext link generation among Web pages, pre-fetching of Web pages to help users to personalize their needs, reducing the waiting time of the users and proxy cache organization. Since clustering process is done on user sessions for each *Entry Page*, the volume of input data is also reduced.

3.8 Publications based on this Chapter

[1] Jeeva Jose, P. Sojan Lal, "Discovery of Similar User Sessions from the Entry Point to a Website", 10th International Conference on ICT and Knowledge Engineering, IEEE, organized by Siam University, Bangkok, Thailand, November 21-23, 2012. ISBN: 978-1-4673-2314-7.

[2] Jeeva Jose, P. Sojan Lal, "Clustering of Users based on Entry Pages to Analyze the deep linked traffic at a Business Organization's Web Site", National Conference on Advanced Computing and Communication Technology, organized by Santhigiri, College of Computer Sciences, Thodupuzha, November 15-16, 2012. ISBN: 978-81-9245-812-0.

>> *End of Chapter 3* <<

Chapter 4: Discovery of User Behavior

The first section of this chapter intends to analyze the user behavior according to sequence length. Sequence length is the depth to which a user navigates in a Website. The analysis helps in setting appropriate commercial marketing strategy. The second section of this chapter is dedicated to identify content and navigational pages of a Website based on reference length. Reference length is the time spent by the user in a Website. Identifying content pages is useful in target advertising which may bring increased revenue to the advertisers. The reference length on each page also leads to the discovery of most preferred content by a user.

4.1 Analysis of Sequence Length

The sequence length of visitors, the depth to which a user visits a Website, can be analyzed to study the behavior of visitors and it may vary depending on the entry point to the Website. A statistical analysis is done to see the differences in sequence length of visitors entered through Home page and other pages. It is also analyzed to see whether sequence length increases in repeated visits. The hypothesis is tested and it revealed that there is a considerable difference in the sequence length of visitors from Home page and other pages. It is observed that sequence length decreases in repeated visits. It is further analyzed to see whether this result varies with time. The analysis helps in setting appropriate commercial marketing strategy.

4.1.1 Background Literature

There are several works in Web Usage Mining. But there are very less works that mentions about the entry points to a Website. Some server log analysis tools like SurfReport and Accure Hitlist mention about most popular *Entry Pages* and most common *Exit Pages* [32Burton01]. A Web Usage Mining tool called SpeedTracer analyses the *Top Ten Entry Pages* [[137]Wu98]. [[139]Plaza09] presents an experiment done with the information that Google Analytics offers for an academic resource about the number of visits on a Website and the traffic source, which includes organic results in search engines, links from referral Web pages or direct access. In other words, it investigates the differences between sessions started by direct connection by typing the site name, by a link on another site, or from a search engine with regard to the behavior and length of sessions. But the only work that analyzes the sequence length is [[100]Ortega10]. No works was found in literature that shows how the sequence length is affected in repeated visits or to further navigation in a Website.

4.1.2 Methodology

Hypothesis is usually considered as the principal instrument in research. A research hypothesis is a predictive statement capable of being tested by scientific methods that relates an independent variable to some dependent variable [[140]Kothari04]. There is null hypothesis generally symbolized as H_0 and alternate hypothesis as H_1. Null hypothesis is the preferred assumption about a population and the hypothesis representing the opposite of null hypothesis is called alternate hypothesis. The null hypothesis and alternate hypothesis are chosen before a sample is drawn. Hypothesis testing helps to decide on the basis of a sample data whether a hypothesis about the population is likely to be true or false. The level of significance usually denoted as α is an important concept in the context of hypothesis testing. The level of significance is the probability with which the null hypothesis H_0 is rejected due to sampling error, though H_0 is true. Usually α is set to 0.05 or else 0.01. Two pre-processed Web log files are used to study the sequence length of visitors. The first one is of a business organization NeST ranging from January 1, 2011 to March 31, 2011 and the second Web log is of an academic institution BPC College ranging from November 1, 2012 to December 31, 2012.

4.1.3 Sequence Length from Entry Point (Case I)

It is intended to see whether there is a significant difference in the sequence length of visitors entering through Home pages with users entering through other pages called deep linking. Let μ_1 represents the mean sequence length of visitors entered into the Website through Home page (population mean) and μ_2 represents the mean sequence length of visitors entered through other pages (population mean). Let $\bar{Y}_1$ denotes the mean sequence length of visitors entered through Home page (sample mean) and sample size is n1. Let $\bar{Y}_2$ denotes the mean sequence length of visitors entered through other pages (sample mean) and sample size is n2. Let the significance level $\alpha = 0.05$.

H_0: $\mu1 = \mu2$. The mean sequence length of users entering through Home page and other pages are equal.

H_1: $\mu1 > \mu2$. The mean sequence length of users entering through Home page is greater than the mean sequence length of users entering through other pages.

This is a Two Sample Test where the population is infinite and the sample size is large. Since the two samples are drawn from the same population, the test static is given by

$$z = \frac{\bar{y}1 - \bar{y}2}{\sqrt{\sigma p^2 \left(\frac{1}{n1} + \frac{1}{n2}\right)}} \qquad (4.1)$$

The population is infinite and σp^2 is not known. Hence σp^2 is replaced by $\sigma S12^2$ [[140]Kothari04] as in equation (4.2).

$$\sigma S12^2 = \frac{n1(\sigma s1^2 + D1^2) + n2(\sigma s2^2 + D2^2)}{n1 + n2} \qquad (4.2)$$

where $D_1 =: \bar{Y}_1 - \bar{Y}_{12}$ and $D_2 = \bar{Y}_2 - \bar{Y}_{12}$.

$$\bar{y}12 = \frac{n1\bar{y}1 + n2\bar{y}2}{n1+n2} \qquad (4.3)$$

Table 4.1 shows various parameters for testing the mean sequence length of visitors through Home page and other pages for data set 1 and Table 4.2 shows various parameters for testing the mean sequence length of visitors through Home page and other pages for data set 2. The calculated z static with a significance level $\alpha = 0.05$ for both data sets falls in the rejection region. Hence H_0 is rejected and alternate hypothesis H_1 is accepted. This is the same for all the three months in data set 1 and for all the two months in data set 2. Fig. 4.1 and Fig. 4.2 shows the temporal information of the mean sequence length of users entered through Home page and other pages for data set 1 and data set 2 respectively.

Table 4.1 Parameters for testing the mean sequence length of visitors through Home page and other pages for data set 1

		January 1-31, 2011	February 1-28, 2011	March 1-31, 2011
1	Number of users entered through Home page, n1	3,806	3,007	3,342
2	Number of users entered through other pages, n2	4,871	4,901	5,088
3	Mean sequence length of users entered through Home pages, $\bar{y}1$	2.7346	2.8141	2.7929
4	Mean sequence length of users entered through other pages, $\bar{y}2$	2.1579	2.1985	2.1801
5	Standard Deviation of n1, $\sigma s1$	2.4119	2.3500	2.3616
6	Standard Deviation of n2, $\sigma s2$	1.9027	2.1242	1.9359
7	Calculated Z Static	12.34	11.90	12.88

Table 4.2 Parameters for testing the mean sequence length of visitors through Home page and other pages for data set 2

		November 1-30, 2012	December 1-31, 2012
1	Number of users entered through home page, n1	741	833
2	Number of users entered through other pages, n2	980	1,156
3	Mean sequence length of users entered through home pages, $\bar{y}_1$	3.5725	4.8958
4	Mean sequence length of users entered through other pages, $\bar{y}_2$	1.8066	2.6190
5	Standard Deviation of n1, σs1	2.7854	2.3412
6	Standard Deviation of n2, σs2	2.1780	2.1553
7	Calculated z static	13.90	20.03

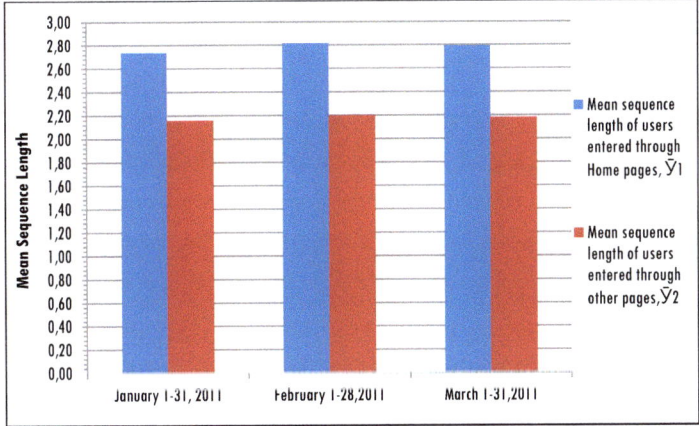

Fig. 4.1 Temporal information of mean sequence length of users entered through Home page and other pages for data set 1

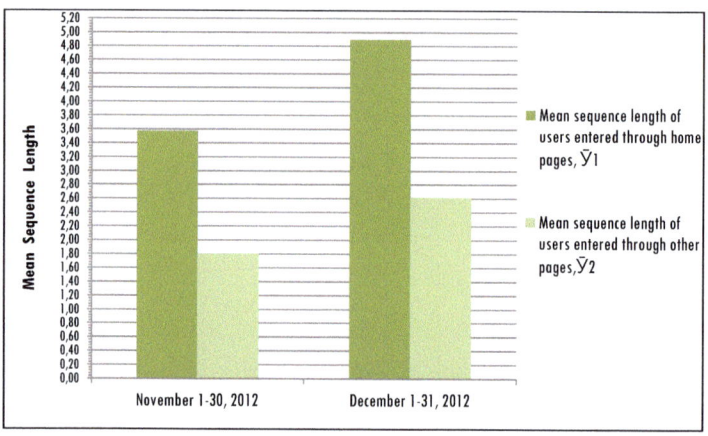

Fig. 4.2 Temporal information of mean sequence length of users entered through Home page and other pages for data set 2

4.1.4 Sequence Length of Repeated Visits (Case II)

It is investigated to see whether there is an increase in the sequence length of visitors in repeated visits. Let μ_1 represents the mean sequence length of single visit (population mean) and μ_2 represents the mean sequence length of repeated visitors (population mean). Let $\bar{Y}_1$ represents the mean sequence length of visitors with single visit and $\bar{Y}_2$ represents the mean sequence length of the repeated visits (sample mean). The first sample size is n1 and second sample size is n2. Let the significance level $\alpha = 0.05$.

H_0: $\mu_1 = \mu_2$. The mean sequence length of users in their single visit and repeated visits are equal.

H_1: $\mu_1 > \mu_2$. The mean sequence length of users in single visit is greater than the mean sequence length of users in repeated visit.

This is also a Two Sample Test where the population is infinite and the sample size is large. Since the two samples are drawn from the same population, the test static can be calculated using equation (4.1). Table 4.3 and Table 4.4 shows various parameters for testing mean sequence length of users with single visit and repeated visits for data set 1 and data set 2 respectively.

Table 4.3 Parameters for testing the mean sequence length of users with single visit and repeated visits for data set 1

		January 1-31, 2011	February 1-28, 2011	March 1-31, 2011
1	Number of users with single visit, n1	6,468	5,992	6,338
2	Number of users with repeated visits, n2	2,209	1,916	2,091
3	Mean sequence length of users with single visit, $\bar{Y}1$	2.7282	2.7366	2.7929
4	Mean sequence length of users with repeated visits, $\bar{Y}2$	1.4817	1.4817	1.5318
5	Standard Deviation of n1, $\sigma s1$	2.3825	2.4522	2.3516
6	Standard Deviation of n2, $\sigma s2$	0.7401	0.7649	0.7567
7	Calculated Z Static	23.4176	21.4113	24.3086

Table 4.4 Parameters for testing the mean sequence length of users with single visit and repeated visits for data set 2

		November 1-30, 2012	December 1-31, 2012
1	Number of users with single visit, n1	976	1,219
2	Number of users with repeated visits, n2	745	770
3	Mean sequence length of users with single visit, $\bar{Y}1$	5.8700	5.6400
4	Mean sequence length of users with repeated visits, $\bar{Y}2$	2.3900	2.4200
5	Standard Deviation of n1, $\sigma s1$	2.8790	2.5489
6	Standard Deviation of n2, $\sigma s2$	2.1234	2.5621
7	Calculated z static	23.06	23.34

The calculated z static with a significance level $\alpha = 0.05$ falls in the rejection region. Hence H_0 is rejected and alternate hypothesis H_1 is accepted. The result is the same for all the three months. Fig. 4.3 shows the temporal information of mean sequence length of users with single visit and repeated visits for data set 1 and Fig. 4.4 shows the temporal information of the mean sequence length of users with single visit and repeated visits for data set 2. The test results of Case I show that the visitors entering the Website through Home page has more sequence length than the users entering through other pages. The test results of Case II show that the sequence length of visitors does not increases in repeated visits. The test for Case I and Case II is done for three months in data set 1 and two months in data set 2 to see whether there is any change in the results. It is the same for all the three months in data set 1 and same for all the two months in data set 2. The temporal information of both the cases is analyzed and it revealed that the results do not vary with time [²³⁹Jose12].

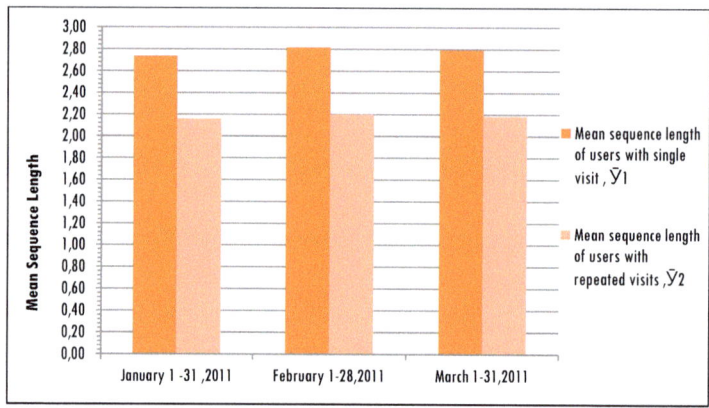

Fig. 4.3 Temporal information of mean sequence length of single visit and repeated visits for data set 1

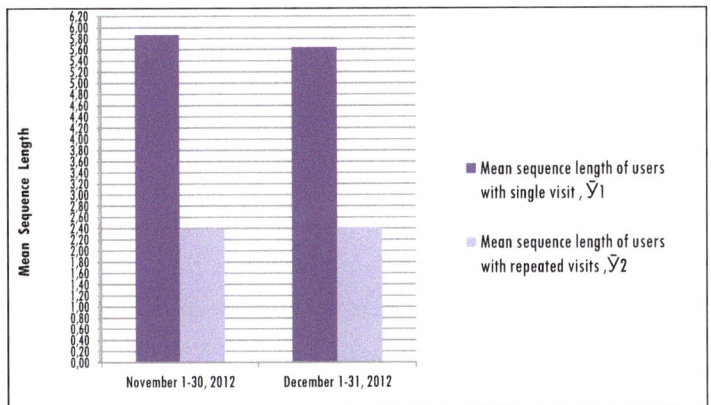

Fig. 4.4 Temporal information of mean sequence length of single visit and repeated visits for data set 2

4.2 Content and Navigational Pages

In a Website, the users may spend different time for viewing different Web pages. The aim is to identify the content and navigational pages in a Website based on rough set approach. It is also studied to see whether the content pages vary with time [236Jose13].

4.2.1 Background Literature

There are several types of Web pages in a Website. The users may spend different time on different pages. Links exist between pages because the Website developer assumes that the pages are related in some way. The Web pages are classified into five main types. The physical characteristics and usage characteristics like in-links from other pages, root of site file structure, out-links, average reference length and maximal forward reference is also studied in [6Cooley99].

- Head Page or Home Page – is a page whose purpose is expected to be the first page that a user visits. It is the page that explains the nature of Website and offer hyperlinks to inner pages. But usually this page may not be the first page that a user visits as there are deep links to a Website or inner pages.

- Content Page – a page that contains a portion of information content that the Website is providing. For sequential pattern mining and association rules these content pages are considered important. The time spend on this page will be higher than the navigational pages. These content pages can give associations between the content pages of a Website.

- Navigational Page – These pages are also known as auxiliary pages whose purpose is to provide links to inner pages or guide users to content pages. These pages have very short viewing time. The purpose of these pages is to facilitate the browsing of user. These pages give essential information about the common traversal paths to a given content page.

- Look Up Page – This is the page usually designed to provide a definition or acronym expansion. There will be usually large number of in-links but few or no out-links. Very little content will be provided by such pages and hence short viewing time.

- Personal Page – This is a low usage page with no common characteristics. Personal pages are expected to be a combination of one of the other page types.

Similarity between Web page accesses based on viewing time is studied in [[121]Chaofeng07]. A hypothetical approach for classifying content and navigational page is done in [[30]Mican09]. [[142]Mobasher99] have presented architecture for automatic Web personalization based on Web usage data, an effective clustering technique using association rule mining to learn overlapping user profiles and discussed how the extracted knowledge can be used in real-time to provide navigational pointers for users to isolate specific types of "content" pages in the recommendation process. For some Websites like Amazon and Ebay, there is a clear separation between content pages and index (navigation) pages. In such cases, it is considered the target pages for a visitor to be exactly the set of content pages requested by the visitor. Other Websites such as information portals or corporate Websites may not have a clear separation between content and index pages [143Srikant01]. A novel concept of fuzzy preference considering the relative access frequency and time durations of a Web page is proposed along with another concept of support considering the absolute access frequency of a Web page to measure Web user interest and preference [144Chen11].

[145Tong07] provides an idea to utilize the duration time of the Web pages to mine Web log and a method for building the Duration Time Frequent Traversal Sequence Tree. [146Yang10] had proposed an algorithm to reduce the number of Web pages of the session sequence and compress the size of frequent traversal sequence by taking the duration time of Web page as a parameter.

4.2.2 Rough Set Theory

There are several works available for the application of rough set theory in diverse domains. Rough set theory has been successfully applied in knowledge acquisition, forecasting, predictive modeling, expert systems and knowledge discovery in databases [147Shan95]. [148Magnani03] have presented a technical report on rough set theory for knowledge discovery in databases. Another important application of rough set theory is illustrated by [149Dimitras99] in which the rough set approach is used to provide a set of rules that is able to discriminate between healthy and failing firms in order to predict business failure. The rough set approach discovers relevant subsets of financial characteristics and represents in these terms all important relationships between the image of a firm and its risk of failure. The method analyses only facts hidden in the input data and communicates with the decision maker in the natural language of rules derived from his/her experience.

[150Pawlak97] explains how rough set theory can be applied to decision making in the presence of uncertainty and vagueness. An efficient rule set generation using rough set theory for classification of high dimensional data is done by [151Gogoi11]. In this, it computes the lower and upper approximation for each concept, then adopts a learning from an algorithm to build concise classification rules for each concept satisfying the given classification accuracy. Lower and upper approximation estimation is designed for the implementation, which substantially reduce the computational complexity of the algorithm. Applying Artificial Intelligence technology and rough set theory for mining association rules to support crime management and fire-fighting resources allocation is illustrated by [152Lee02].

Association rule algorithms often generate an excessive number of rules, many of which are not significant. It is difficult to determine which rules are more useful, interesting and important. [153Li05] has introduced a rough set based process by which a rule importance measure is calculated for association rules to select the most appropriate rules. A rule based classification algorithm using rough set approach is proposed by [154Liao12]. [155Sabu11] has proposed rule induction using rough set theory which was applied in agriculture. An indiscernibility relation I(B) is defined for every rough set theory. The two operations on sets X C U are as follows.

$B_*(X) = \{ x \in U: B(x) \subset X \}$,

$B^*(X) = \{ x \in U: B(x) \cap X \neq \phi \}$,

The above two operations are assigned to every subset X of the Universe U the two sets $B_*(X)$ and $B^*(X)$ called the B-lower and B-upper approximation of X respectively. $B^*(X) - B_*(X)$ is referred to as the boundary region of X assigning to every subset X of the Universe U the two sets $B_*(X)$ and $B^*(X)$ called the B-lower and B-upper approximation of X respectively. Fig 4.5 shows the Rough set concept with lower approximation, upper approximation and boundary regions of X.

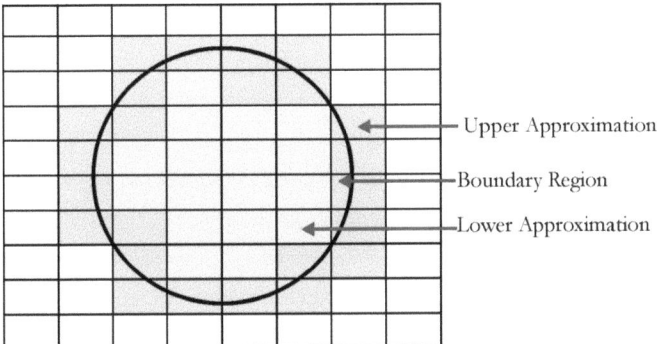

Fig. 4.5 Rough set concept with lower approximation, upper approximation and boundary regions of X

4.2.3 Identifying Content and Navigational Pages

For identifying the content and navigational pages in a Website, the log file of a business organization NeST ranging from January 1 to February 28, 2011 is used. The log files are cleaned and pre-processed to identify user sessions. The different pages traversed by the user and corresponding viewing time for each page is obtained. Viewing time for each page is calculated as follows. Let $P_1, P_2, P_3, \ldots P_n$ be the pages accessed by the user in a session. Let t_1 represents the time for page P_1 in log and t_2 represents the time for page P_2.

Then the viewing time t_{view} for page P_1 is calculated as the difference between two consecutive viewing times.

$$t_{view} = t_2 - t_1 \qquad (4.4)$$

But for the last page in each user session the viewing time is not available as it is difficult to identify when the user has left the Website. In the proposed approach, rough set theory is used to identify content and navigational pages. This approach is used because certain pages may serve as both content and navigational pages. A threshold needs to be fixed for identifying content and navigational pages. If the mean viewing time of pages is used to fix the threshold, then there will be a great difference in the result because the difference between minimum and maximum viewing time will be very large.

Hence the percentile concept is chosen to fix the threshold. This method is most suited when the data size is very large. Percentiles are the values which divide the series into 100 equal parts. Obviously, there are 99 percentiles P_1, P_2, P_3, P_{99} such that $P_1 < P_2 <, P_3, <P_{99}$. Percentiles are especially useful in scaling and ranking of test scores in psychological and educational statistics [141 Nair01]. We have calculated the twenty fifth percentile as

$$P25 = Size\ of\ 25\left(\frac{N+1}{100}\right) item \qquad (4.5)$$

All the pages with viewing time above P_{25} is considered for identifying content pages. The pages with all viewing time below P_{25} is considered as pure navigational pages with short viewing time. Similarly the seventy fifth percentile is calculated as

$$P75 = Size\ of\ 75\left(\frac{N+1}{100}\right) item \qquad (4.6)$$

The pages in lower approximation $B_*(X)$ and upper approximation $B^*(X)$ are defined as

$$B_*(X) = \{\ x\ \epsilon\ U: B(x)\ C\ X,\ where\ X >= P_{75}\ \} \qquad (4.7)$$
$$B^*(X) = \{\ x\ \epsilon\ U: B(x) \cap X \neq \phi,\ where\ X >= P_{25}\} \qquad (4.8)$$

The central point of rough set theory is the notion of set approximation. Any set in U can be approximated by its lower and upper approximation. The pages with only one viewing time is removed because pages with only one viewing time is not sufficient for classifying it as content or navigational page. Algorithm 4.1 shows rough set approach for identifying content and navigational pages and Fig. 4.6 shows the Process Flow Diagram for identifying content and navigational pages.

Input: A pre-processed Web log file with pages and different viewing times for each page.

Output: A file with content pages (lower approximation), content pages (upper approximation) and navigational pages.

Method:
```
Begin
  Open the Pre-processed file with pages and viewing times
  Set the threshold for lower approximation as P75 and upper
  approximation as P25
  Do While not EOF()
    For each page Pi
      IF ALL viewing time tview of page Pi >=P75
        Add Pi to lower approximation
      EndIF
      IF ALL viewing time tview of page Pi >=P25
        Add Pi to upper approximation
      EndIF
      IF ALL viewing time tview of page Pi < P25
        Add Pi to Navigational pages
      EndIF
    EndFor
  EndDo
  Close file
End
```

Algorithm 4.1 Rough set approach for identifying content and navigational pages

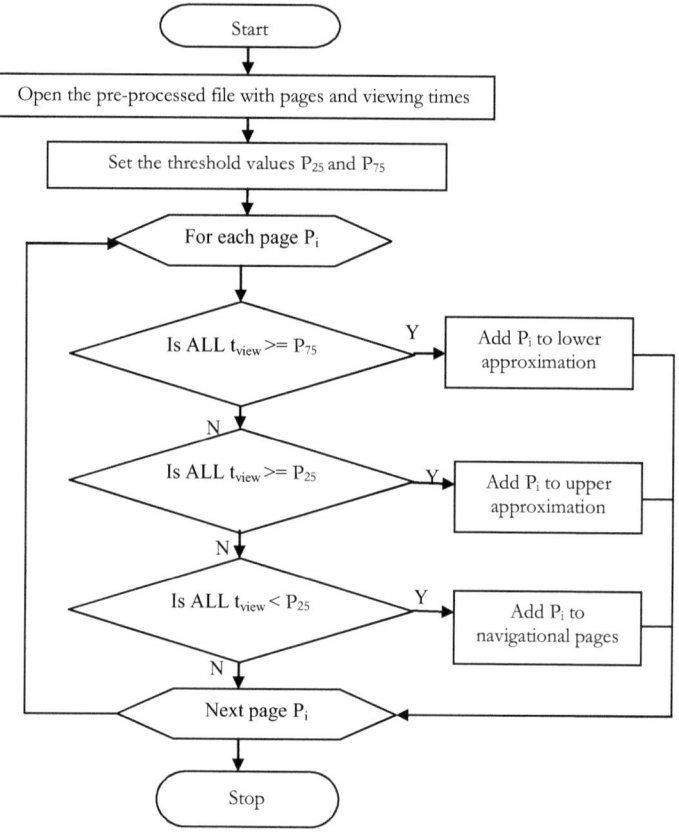

Fig. 4.6 Process Flow Diagram for identifying content and navigational pages

Table 4.5 shows the result of rough set approach for identifying content and navigational pages for data set 1 and Table 4.6 shows the result of rough set approach for identifying content and navigational pages for data set 2.

Table 4.5 Results of rough set approach for identifying content and navigational pages for data set 1

		January 1-31, 2011	February 1-28, 2011
1	Total no: of pages in the log	499	380
2	No: of pages after removing single viewing time	198	168
3	No: of navigational pages	68	57
4	No: of content pages (upper approximation)	119	103
5	No: of content pages (lower approximation)	11	8

Table 4.6 Results of rough set approach for identifying content and navigational pages for data set 2

		November 1-30, 2012	December 1-31, 2012
1	Total no: of pages in the log	378	401
2	No: of pages after removing single viewing time	151	168
3	No: of navigational pages	119	125
4	No: of content pages (upper approximation)	26	34
5	No: of content pages (lower approximation)	6	9

Fig. 4.7 shows the graphical representation of content and navigational pages for data set 1 and Fig. 4.8 shows the graphical representation of content and navigational pages for data set 2.

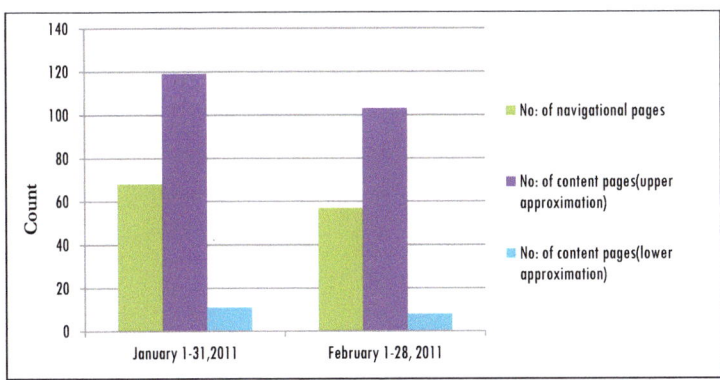

Fig. 4.7 Graphical representation of content and navigational pages for data set 1

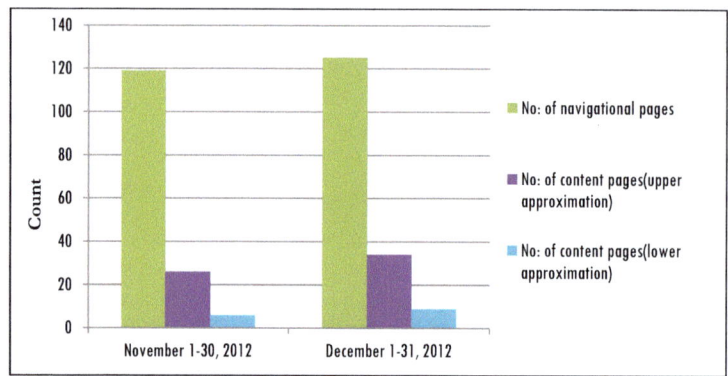

Fig. 4.8 Graphical representation of content and navigational pages for data set 2

Lower Approximation: The pages in lower approximation falls in the category of potential pages which are termed as content pages. For all the users these pages have the maximum viewing time. These pages can be used for target advertising or to promote the key features of the organization. Table 4.7 shows pages in lower approximation (content pages) for data set 1 ranging from January 1 to 31, 2011. Table 4.9 shows pages in lower approximation (content pages) for data set 2 ranging from November 1 to 30, 2012.

Upper approximation: The pages in upper approximation serve as both content and navigational pages. These pages may tend to be potential pages. The pages which do not belong to the upper approximation and lower approximations are purely navigational pages. Table 4.8 shows the pages in upper approximation that served as both content and navigational pages for one month ranging from January 1 to 31, 2011 for data set 1. Similarly Table 4.10 shows the pages in upper approximation that served as both content and navigational pages for one month ranging from November 1 to 30, 2012 for data set 2.

Table 4.7 Pages in lower approximation (content pages) for data set 1

	January 1-31, 2011
1	/index.php?Itemid=73&id=71&option=com_content&task=view
2	/index.php?Itemid=8&id=5&option=com_content&task=view
3	/index.php?Itemid=91&id=2&option=com_content&task=view
4	/index.php?Itemid=92&id=104&option=com_content&task=view
5	/index.php?Itemid=95&id=6&option=com_content&task=view
6	/index.php?option=com_content&task=view&id=105&Itemid=94
7	/index.php?option=com_content&task=view&id=140
8	/index.php?option=com_content&task=view&id=153&Itemid=160
9	/index.php?option=com_content&task=view&id=173&Itemid=94
10	/index.php?option=com_content&task=view&id=40&Itemid=43
11	/index.php?option=com_content&task=view&id=52&Itemid=52

Table 4.8 Pages in upper approximation (content and navigational pages) for data set 1

	January-1-31, 2011		
1	Home Page	61	/index.php?option=com_content&task=view&id=33&Itemid=98
2	/index.php	62	/index.php?option=com_content&task=view&id=35&Itemid=38
3	/index.php?Itemid=118&option=com_joomap	63	/index.php?option=com_content&task=view&id=35&Itemid=99
4	/index.php?Itemid=20&id=19&option=com_content&task=view	64	/index.php?option=com_content&task=view&id=39&Itemid=42
5	/index.php?Itemid=28&id=26&option=com_content&task=view	65	/index.php?option=com_content&task=view&id=4&Itemid=106
6	/index.php?Itemid=3&id=3&option=com_content&task=view	66	/index.php?option=com_content&task=view&id=4&Itemid=7
7	/index.php?Itemid=3&id=3&option=com_content&task=view	67	/index.php?option=com_content&task=view&id=44&Itemid=46
8	/index.php?Itemid=38&id=35&option=com_content&task=view	68	/index.php?option=com_content&task=view&id=45&Itemid=101
9	/index.php?Itemid=46&id=44&option=com_content&task=view	69	/index.php?option=com_content&task=view&id=45&Itemid=47
10	/index.php?Itemid=72&id=70&option=com_content&task=view	70	/index.php?option=com_content&task=view&id=46&Itemid=48
11	/index.php?Itemid=85&id=101&option=com_content&task=view	71	/index.php?option=com_content&task=view&id=48&Itemid=49
12	/index.php?option=com_content&task=blogcategory&id=103&Itemid=104	72	/index.php?option=com_content&task=view&id=49&Itemid=50
13	/index.php?option=com_content&task=blogcategory&id=103&Itemid=111	73	/index.php?option=com_content&task=view&id=5&Itemid=8
14	/index.php?option=com_content&task=blogcategory&id=103&Itemid=94	74	/index.php?option=com_content&task=view&id=5&Itemid=90
15	/index.php?option=com_content&task=view&id=10&Itemid=13	75	/index.php?option=com_content&task=view&id=50&Itemid=102
16	/index.php?option=com_content&task=view&id=101&Itemid=85	76	/index.php?option=com_content&task=view&id=50&Itemid=51
17	/index.php?option=com_content&task=view&id=101&Itemid=93	77	/index.php?option=com_content&task=view&id=51&Itemid=54
18	/index.php?option=com_content&task=view&id=102&Itemid=84	78	/index.php?option=com_content&task=view&id=54&Itemid=103
19	/index.php?option=com_content&task=view&id=103&Itemid=86	79	/index.php?option=com_content&task=view&id=54&Itemid=55
20	/index.php?option=com_content&task=view&id=104&Itemid=87	80	/index.php?option=com_content&task=view&id=55&Itemid=56
21	/index.php?option=com_content&task=view&id=104&Itemid=92	81	/index.php?option=com_content&task=view&id=56&Itemid=57
22	/index.php?option=com_content&task=view&id=11&Itemid=14	82	/index.php?option=com_content&task=view&id=57&Itemid=58
23	/index.php?option=com_content&task=view&id=110&Itemid=113	83	/index.php?option=com_content&task=view&id=58&Itemid=59
24	/index.php?option=com_content&task=view&id=111&Itemid=114	84	/index.php?option=com_content&task=view&id=59&Itemid=108
25	/index.php?option=com_content&task=view&id=128&Itemid=15	85	/index.php?option=com_content&task=view&id=59&Itemid=61
26	/index.php?option=com_content&task=view&id=13&Itemid=16	86	/index.php?option=com_content&task=view&id=6&Itemid=9
27	/index.php?option=com_content&task=view&id=134	87	/index.php?option=com_content&task=view&id=6&Itemid=95
28	/index.php?option=com_content&task=view&id=14&Itemid=17	88	/index.php?option=com_content&task=view&id=60&Itemid=109

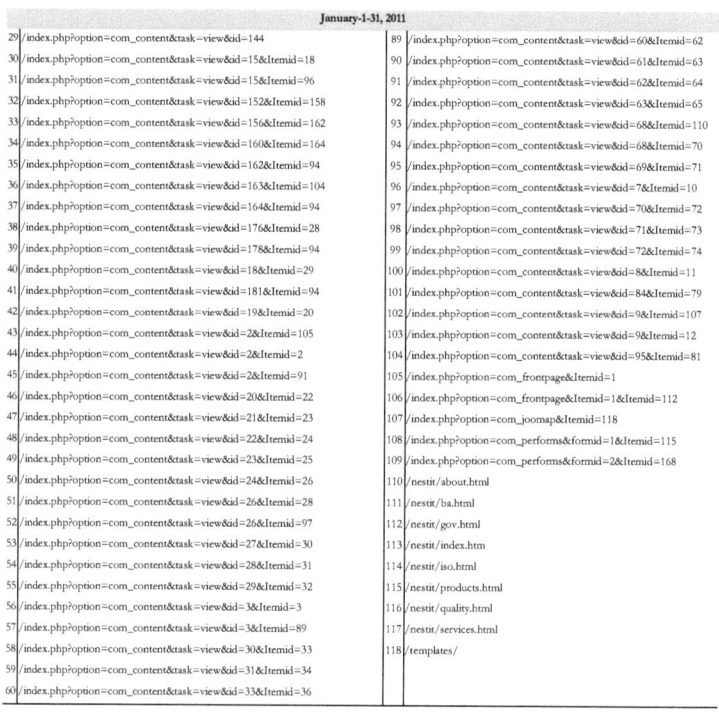

January 1-31, 2011	
29 /index.php?option=com_content&task=view&id=144	89 /index.php?option=com_content&task=view&id=60&Itemid=62
30 /index.php?option=com_content&task=view&id=15&Itemid=18	90 /index.php?option=com_content&task=view&id=61&Itemid=63
31 /index.php?option=com_content&task=view&id=15&Itemid=96	91 /index.php?option=com_content&task=view&id=62&Itemid=64
32 /index.php?option=com_content&task=view&id=152&Itemid=158	92 /index.php?option=com_content&task=view&id=63&Itemid=65
33 /index.php?option=com_content&task=view&id=156&Itemid=162	93 /index.php?option=com_content&task=view&id=68&Itemid=110
34 /index.php?option=com_content&task=view&id=160&Itemid=164	94 /index.php?option=com_content&task=view&id=68&Itemid=70
35 /index.php?option=com_content&task=view&id=162&Itemid=94	95 /index.php?option=com_content&task=view&id=69&Itemid=71
36 /index.php?option=com_content&task=view&id=163&Itemid=104	96 /index.php?option=com_content&task=view&id=7&Itemid=10
37 /index.php?option=com_content&task=view&id=164&Itemid=94	97 /index.php?option=com_content&task=view&id=70&Itemid=72
38 /index.php?option=com_content&task=view&id=176&Itemid=28	98 /index.php?option=com_content&task=view&id=71&Itemid=73
39 /index.php?option=com_content&task=view&id=178&Itemid=94	99 /index.php?option=com_content&task=view&id=72&Itemid=74
40 /index.php?option=com_content&task=view&id=18&Itemid=29	100 /index.php?option=com_content&task=view&id=8&Itemid=11
41 /index.php?option=com_content&task=view&id=181&Itemid=94	101 /index.php?option=com_content&task=view&id=84&Itemid=79
42 /index.php?option=com_content&task=view&id=19&Itemid=20	102 /index.php?option=com_content&task=view&id=9&Itemid=107
43 /index.php?option=com_content&task=view&id=2&Itemid=105	103 /index.php?option=com_content&task=view&id=9&Itemid=12
44 /index.php?option=com_content&task=view&id=2&Itemid=2	104 /index.php?option=com_content&task=view&id=95&Itemid=81
45 /index.php?option=com_content&task=view&id=2&Itemid=91	105 /index.php?option=com_frontpage&Itemid=1
46 /index.php?option=com_content&task=view&id=20&Itemid=22	106 /index.php?option=com_frontpage&Itemid=1&Itemid=112
47 /index.php?option=com_content&task=view&id=21&Itemid=23	107 /index.php?option=com_joomap&Itemid=118
48 /index.php?option=com_content&task=view&id=22&Itemid=24	108 /index.php?option=com_performs&formid=1&Itemid=115
49 /index.php?option=com_content&task=view&id=23&Itemid=25	109 /index.php?option=com_performs&formid=2&Itemid=168
50 /index.php?option=com_content&task=view&id=24&Itemid=26	110 /nestit/about.html
51 /index.php?option=com_content&task=view&id=26&Itemid=28	111 /nestit/ba.html
52 /index.php?option=com_content&task=view&id=26&Itemid=97	112 /nestit/gov.html
53 /index.php?option=com_content&task=view&id=27&Itemid=30	113 /nestit/index.htm
54 /index.php?option=com_content&task=view&id=28&Itemid=31	114 /nestit/iso.html
55 /index.php?option=com_content&task=view&id=29&Itemid=32	115 /nestit/products.html
56 /index.php?option=com_content&task=view&id=3&Itemid=3	116 /nestit/quality.html
57 /index.php?option=com_content&task=view&id=3&Itemid=89	117 /nestit/services.html
58 /index.php?option=com_content&task=view&id=30&Itemid=33	118 /templates/
59 /index.php?option=com_content&task=view&id=31&Itemid=34	
60 /index.php?option=com_content&task=view&id=33&Itemid=36	

Table 4.9 Pages in lower approximation (content pages) for data set 2

	November 1-30, 2012
1	/courses.php
2	/ragging_prohibition.php
3	/newscontent_arc.php
4	/phy_edu_abt.php
5	/photo_gallery.php
6	/research_minor.php

Table 4.10 Pages in upper approximation (content and navigational pages) for data set 2

November 1-30, 2012	
1 Home page	14 /mal_fac.php
2 /fees_structure.php	15 /law_fac.php
3 /iqac.php	16 /physics_abt.php
4 /computerapp_abt.php	17 /clubs_nss.php
5 /rules.php	18 /hin_fac.php
6 /admission.php	19 /research_major.php
7 /index.php	20 /fac_details.php?dept=MATHS&id=19
8 /electronics_abt.php	21 /fac_details.php?dept=BSCE&id=24
9 /journ_abt.php	22 /newsContent.php?newsId=49
10 /college_bus.php	23 /evaluation.php
11 /admission.php	24 /fac_details.php?dept=BCA&id=6
12 /healthy.php	25 /fac_details.php?dept=MSCEIN&id=51
13 /library_staff.php	26 /nrc.php

4.2.4 Temporal Analysis of Content and Navigational Pages

Analysis is done to see whether the number of content pages and navigational pages changes with time. For this, the process is repeatedly done for the Web log data of data set 1 ranging from February 1 to 28, 2011 and for data set 2, it is done for one more month ranging from December 1 to 31, 2012. It is found that the number of navigational pages, number of content pages both in lower and upper approximation changes with time for both data sets. The pages in lower and upper approximation also vary with time in both data sets. Table 4.11 and Table 4.12 shows temporal analysis of pages in lower approximation (content pages) for data set 1 and data set 2 respectively.

Table 4.11 Temporal analysis of the pages in lower approximation (content pages) for data set 1

	January 1-31, 2011	February 1-28, 2011
1	/index.php?Itemid=73&id=71&option=com_content&task=view	/index.php?Itemid=73&id=71&option=com_content&task=view
2	/index.php?Itemid=8&id=5&option=com_content&task=view	/index.php?Itemid=8&id=5&option=com_content&task=view
3	/index.php?Itemid=91&id=2&option=com_content&task=view	/index.php?Itemid=91&id=2&option=com_content&task=view
4	/index.php?Itemid=92&id=104&option=com_content&task=view	/index.php?option=com_content&task=view&id=140
5	/index.php?Itemid=95&id=6&option=com_content&task=view	/index.php?option=com_content&task=view&id=40&Itemid=43
6	/index.php?option=com_content&task=view&id=105&Itemid=94	/index.php?option=com_content&task=blogcategory&id=103&Itemid=104
7	/index.php?option=com_content&task=view&id=140	/index.php?Itemid=20&id=19&option=com_content&task=view
8	/index.php?option=com_content&task=view&id=153&Itemid=160	/index.php?Itemid=28&id=26&option=com_content&task=view
9	/index.php?option=com_content&task=view&id=173&Itemid=94	
10	/index.php?option=com_content&task=view&id=40&Itemid=43	
11	/index.php?option=com_content&task=view&id=52&Itemid=52	

Table 4.12 Temporal analysis of the pages in lower approximation (content pages) for data set 2

	November 1-30, 2012	December 1-31, 2012
1	/courses.php	/courses.php
2	/ragging_prohibition.php	/ragging_prohibition.php
3	/newscontent_arc.php	/clubs_vings.php
4	/phy_edu_abt.php	/profile.php
5	/photo_gallery.php	/photo_gallery.php
6	/research_minor.php	/phy_edu_abt.php
7		/baselios_poulose.php
8		/location.php
9		/contactus.php

4.3 Conclusion

It is observed that the sequence length of visitors entered through Home page is more than that of visitors entered through other pages. Hence Website owners can think of a search engine optimization policy. The users entering through Home page may know the URL and architecture of the site. Hence they may go deep while users entering through other pages (deep linking) may reach at the Website by a keyword search using search engines. They may quit the site after visiting a particular page. The decrease in sequence length of repeated visits shows that they are particular in accessing the required page and may not explore the site in deep. This study is important because many business and E-commerce organizations have put their product catalogues and databases on the Web. A large number of users are accessing internet based solutions and many more are expected to follow. Hence the sequence length, entry point and repeated visits are important while studying the behavior of users. The visitors can be identified especially from a particular demographic for marketing purposes. The frequently traversed path from entry points can be studied to see the most preferred content by the Web users.

Classification of content and navigational pages is yet another application of rough set theory to identify potential pages. The results of this approach could be used for target advertising because advertisers seek to post their advertisements on content pages especially pages in lower approximation. This also aids to identify the most preferred content by a user because users spent more time on potential pages. Identifying content pages is very crucial in association rule mining and discovery of frequent patterns. This work can be extended to see whether the navigational pages of different users change to content pages in repeated visits.

Two case studies using the data set from NeST and BPC mentioned in Section 4.1.2 have been done to identify the mean sequence length of visitors entered through Home page and other pages which is depicted in Fig. 4.1 and Fig. 4.2 respectively. This result can be successfully used for search engine optimization [[239]Jose12] such as optimizing the title tags of the Home page, optimizing the filenames of the images in Home page, optimizing the content of the Home page and meta tags with popularly used keywords.

Similarly the two case studies have been done to identify the mean sequence length of single visits and repeated visits of the users which is shown in Fig 4.3 and Fig 4.4. This result can be used for better customer relationship management including customer retention. The identified repeated visitors can be retained by offering discounts, personalized services and ask for opinions for their satisfaction.

For classifying content and navigational pages, two Web logs are used and the results are shown in Table 4.7 and Table 4.9 respectively. The result of the classification is useful in deciding the advertising strategy which is mentioned in [[236]Jose13].

4.4 Publications based on this Chapter

[1] Jeeva Jose, P. Sojan Lal, "A Rough Set Approach to Identify Content and Navigational Pages at a Website", Proceedings of the IEEE International Multi Conference on Automation, Computing, Control, Communication and Compressed Sensing, organized by St. Joseph's College of Engineering Pala, March 22-23, 2013. ISBN: 978-1-4673-5089-1.

[2] Jeeva Jose, P. Sojan Lal, "Analysis of the Sequence Length of Visitors from the Entry Point and their Repeated Visits", Proceedings of the International Conference on Data Science and Engineering, IEEE, organized by Department of Computer Science, CUSAT, Cochin, July 18-20, 2012, pp.179-183. ISBN: 978-1-4673-2146-4.

>> *End of Chapter 4* <<

Chapter 5: Identification of Search Engine Crawler Behavior

Web Log Mining is mostly done for the extraction of user behavior from Web log data. The log files also provide immense information about search engine traffic at a Website. These search engine traffic is helpful to analyze the ethics of search engines, quality of the crawlers, periodicity of the visits of crawlers and also the server load. This chapter discovers the differences in search engine crawler behavior in terms of the number of visits, pages crawled, time spent and the time delay between two consecutive visits.

5.1 Introduction

A Web search engine consists of three parts.

1) A crawler that retrieves Web pages to be put into the engine's collection of Web pages.

2) An indexer that builds the inverted index (also called the index), which is the main data structure used by the search engine and represents the crawled Web pages.

3) A query handler that answers user queries using the index [[178]Henzinger03].

Search engine crawlers are automated programs which periodically visit a Website to update information. Crawlers are also known as 'bots', 'spiders', or 'robots'. Crawlers are the main components of a search engine and without them the Websites will not be listed in search results. The visibility of the Websites depends on the quality of the crawlers. Search engines such as Google periodically use Web robots to grab all the pages from a Website to update their search indexes. If the site doesn't attract many visitors, the number of requests from all the Web robots that have visited the site might exceed that of human generated requests [^{180}Tanasa04].

Search engines do not index sites equally, may not index new pages for months, and no engine indexes more than about 16% of the Web [^{213}Lawrence99]. Certain crawlers avoid too much load on a server by crawling the server at a low speed during peak hours of the day and at a high speed during late night and early morning. A crawler for a large search engine has to address two issues.

1) It has to have a good crawling strategy which means a strategy for deciding which pages to download next.
2) It needs to have a highly optimized system architecture that can download a large number of pages per second while being robust against crashes, manageable of resources and Web servers [^{214}Shkapenyuk02].

The Web creates new challenges for information retrieval. The amount of information on the Web is growing rapidly as well as the number of new users inexperienced in the art of Web search. There are several works in literature which have studied about the design and behavior of search engine crawlers. [^{166}Brin98] provides a detailed anatomy of the large hyper textual Web search engine, Google. It explains the design goals, system features, scalability, improved search quality, the PageRank calculation, the detailed overview of its architecture, data structures, performance and comparison with other crawlers. PageRank is the backbone of Google.

Web Mining tasks include mining Web search engine data, analyzing Web's link structures, classifying Web documents automatically, mining Web page semantic structures and page contents, mining Web dynamics (mining log files), building a multilayered and multidimensional Web. Web log data is usually mined to study the user behavior at Websites. It also contains immense information about the search engine traffic contributed by crawlers. The user traffic is removed by pre-processing tasks, otherwise it may bias the search engine behavior. Thus the refined data enables to analyze search engine crawler behavior. The search engine crawler is an important module of a Web search engine and the quality of a crawler directly affects the searching quality of Web search engines.

The process of identifying the Web crawlers is important because they can generate 90% of the traffic on Websites [[30]Mican09]. Commercial search engines play a vital role in accessing Websites and wider information dissemination [[156]Sullivan03][[157]Vaughan04]. A typical crawler starts with a seed set of pages. It then downloads these pages, extracts hyperlinks and crawls pages pointed to by these new hyperlinks. The crawler repeats this step until there are no more pages to crawl or some resources (e.g. time or network bandwidth) are exhausted [[161]Brandman00]. These crawlers are highly automated and seldom regulated manually [[158]Bhagwani11] [[159]Schwenke06] [[160]Thelwall01] [[172]Chatterjee01].

The crawlers periodically visit the Websites to update the content. Certain Websites like stock market sites or online news may need frequent crawling to update the search engine repositories. Web crawlers access the Websites for diverse purpose which includes security violations also. Hence they may lead to ethical issues like privacy, security and blocking of server access. Crawling activities can be regulated from the server side with the help of Robots Exclusion Protocol [[165]Sun07]. This protocol is present in a file called robots.txt [[183]Yu05][[219]Koster95] . Robots.txt is a file that Web agents (crawlers) check for information on how the site is to be catalogued. It is a text file that defines what documents and/or directories are forbidden which are followed by ethical crawlers. There is also an option to direct the Web agents (crawlers) per page.

Every HTML document contains a heading section in which meta-data about the document (like keywords, a description of the content, and so on) can be included. Such sections are called 'meta tags.' Within the meta-tags of each

HTML document one can specify whether or not a robot is allowed to index the page and submit it to a search engine. Some robots will simply ignore the meta-tags because of the fact that those tags are often misused by page owners who want to get a higher ranking in a search index [[179]Wel04].

Robots (crawlers) may also ignore the robots.txt file or purposely load the documents that the file marks as disallowed. But it is also possible to crawl the pages at a Website without accessing the robots.txt. Certain crawlers seems to disobey the rules in robots.txt after its modification because crawlers like "Googlebot", "Slurp" , "MSNbot" cache the robots.txt file for a Website [[162]Drott02]. Usually ethical crawlers first access this file which will be present at the root directory of the Website and follow the rules specified by robots.txt [[162]Drott02][[163]Giles10]. Certain pages and folders are denied access because they contain sensitive information which is not intended to be publically available. There may be situations where two or more versions of a page will be available one as html and other one as pdf. The crawlers can be made to avoid crawling the pdf version for eliminating redundant crawling. Also certain files like JavaScripts, images, stylesheets etc. can be avoided for saving the time and bandwidth. The structure of a robots.txt file is follows.

User-agent:

Disallow:

"User-agent:" is the search engine crawler and "Disallow:" lists the files and directories to be excluded from indexing. In addition to "User-agent:" and "Disallow:" entries, comment lines are included by putting the # sign at the beginning of the line. For example all user agents are disallowed from accessing the folder /a. This is given in robots.txt as follows.

```
# All user agents are disallowed to see the /a folder.
User-agent: *
Disallow: /a/
```

The Website monitoring software Google Analytics does not track crawlers or bots. This is because Google Analytics tracking is activated by a JavaScript that is placed on every page of the Website. A crawler hardly recognizes these scripts and hence the visits from search engines are not recognized.

5.2 Background Literature

Search engines largely rely on Web crawlers to collect information from the Web. Due to the unregulated open-access nature of the Web, crawler activities are extremely diverse. Such crawling activities can be regulated from the server side by deploying the Robots Exclusion Protocol in a file called robots.txt. The study of robots.txt is done in [[165]Sun07][[167]Drott98]. Current day crawlers retrieve content only from the publicly indexable Web. This includes the set of Web pages reachable purely by following hypertext links, ignoring search forms and pages that require authorization or prior registration. In particular, they ignore the tremendous amount of high quality content "hidden" behind search forms, in large searchable electronic databases.

[[168]Raghavan00] has provided a framework for addressing the problem of extracting content from this hidden Web. Scalable Web crawlers are an important component of many Web services. Building a scalable crawler is a non-trivial endeavor because the data manipulated by the crawler is too big to fit entirely in memory, so there are performance issues relating to how to balance the use of disk and memory. [[169]Heydon99] has enumerated the main components required in any scalable crawler and it has discussed design alternatives for those components. In particular, it has described *Mercator*, an extensible scalable crawler written entirely in Java. *Mercator's* design features a crawler core for handling the main crawling tasks. Extensibility is achieved through protocol and processing modules.

The traditional information retrieval measures of recall and precision at varying numbers of retrieved documents were calculated and used these as the basis for statistical comparisons of retrieval effectiveness among the eight search engines [[170]Gordon99]. [[171]Sullivan13] has conducted a study on major search engines and directories and cites why these search engines are the toppers in the list.

[[161]Brandman00] has proposed the need for Web servers to export meta data describing their pages so that crawlers can efficiently create and maintain large, fresh repositories. This meta-data includes the last modified date and size for each available file which if exported could save considerable amount of band width [[188]Engler08].[[173]Thelwall01] reports on an experiment to investigate the effect of link count on the indexing of 1000 sites in three search portals over a period of seven months. It was found that, although all search engines added sites during the period of the survey, only Google showed evidence of being very responsive to the existence of links on the test site, whereas AltaVista's results were very stable over time. Due to limited bandwidth, computational resources and dynamic nature of the Web, search engines cannot index every Web page and even the covered pages cannot be monitored continuously for changes. It is important to develop crawling strategies to prioritize the pages to be indexed. For topic specific search engine crawlers, this is more important.

[[174]Menczer01] has proposed three different methods to evaluate crawling strategies and proposed metrics is applied to compare three topic-driven crawling algorithms based on similarity ranking, link analysis and adaptive agents.[[175]Chen01] have introduced MetaSpider, a meta-search engine that has real-time indexing and categorizing functions. It is shown that MetaSpider performs better in precision when compared with several widely used meta-search systems. Because of its built-in automatic indexing and categorizing components, MetaSpider greatly reduces the manual effort required by the user for Web searching and browsing. [[176]Chau01] introduced CI Spider and Meta

Spider which can potentially facilitate the Web searching process for internet users with different needs by using a personalized approach. The results also demonstrated that powerful AI techniques such as noun phrasing and SOM can be processed on the user's personal computer to perform further analysis on Web search results, which allows the user to understand the search topic more correctly and completely.

[177Thelwall02] have compared five different previously used Web survey methodologies, conducted a simple experiment that demonstrates concrete differences between them and a new hybrid random page selection methodology is also introduced. [181Papapetrou04] has described IPMicra, a distributed location aware Web crawler that utilizes an IP address hierarchy and allows crawling of links in a near optimal location aware manner. The crawler outperforms earlier distributed crawling approaches without a significant overhead. [182Ntoulas04] focus on aspects of potential interest to search engine designers: the evolution of link structure over time, the rate of creation of new pages, new distinct content on the Web and the rate of change of the content of existing pages under search-centric measures of degree of change which eventually leads to the design of effective search engines. [184Srinivasan05] has proposed a framework which is effective at evaluating, comparing, differentiating and interpreting the performance of the four topical crawlers namely InfoSpider, Breadth First Search1 (BFS1), Breadth First Search256 (BFS256) and Breadth First. [185Jansen06] have compared interactions occurring between users and Web search engines from the perspectives of session length, query length, query complexity and content viewed among the Web search engines. The above research shows the following results.

1) Users are viewing fewer result pages.
2) Searchers on United States of America based Web search engines use more query operators than searchers on European based search engines.

3) There are statistically significant differences in the use of Boolean operators and result pages viewed.
4) One cannot necessarily apply results from studies of one particular Web search engine to another Web search engine.

Backup of Websites is often not considered until after a catastrophic event has occurred to either the Website or its Webmaster. [186McCown06] has introduced "lazy preservation" – digital preservation performed as a result of the normal operation of Web crawlers and caches. Lazy preservation is a best effort, wide coverage digital preservation service that may be used as a last resort when Website backups are unavailable. Web repositories may not crawl orphan pages, protected pages, very large pages, pages deep in a Web collection or links influenced by JavaScript, Flash or session IDs. If a Web repository will not or cannot crawl and cache a resource, it cannot be recovered. They have also measured the ability of Google, MSN and Yahoo to cache four synthetic Web collections over a period of four months. The use of data stored in transaction logs of Web search engines, Intranets and Websites can provide valuable insight into understanding the information searching process of online searchers. This understanding can enlighten information system design, interface development and devising the information architecture for content collections. [187Jansen06] has presented a review and foundation for conducting Web search transaction log analysis. [189Nath11] has addressed the problem of bandwidth consumption by introducing an efficient indexing system based on mobile crawlers. The proposed system employs mobile agents to crawl the pages. These mobile agent based crawlers retrieve the pages, process them, compare their data to filter out pages that are not modified after last crawl and then compress them before sending them to the search engine for indexing.

[190Dikaiakos05] has analyzed crawler requests to derive insights into the behavior and strategy of crawlers. They have proposed a set of simple metrics that describe qualitative characteristics of crawler behavior, compared with a crawler's preference on resources of a particular format, its frequency of visits on a Website and the pervasiveness of its visits to a particular site. For that work, Web-server access logs from five academic sites in three different countries were used. Based on those logs, the activity of different crawlers that belongs to five search engines: Google, AltaVista, Inktomi, FastSearch and CiteSeer were analyzed.

5.3 Pre-processing

In our work the log files of 2 different organizations are selected for study. The first data set is the log file of a business organization NeST ranging from April 1, 2011 to May 31, 2011 and second data set belongs to an academic Website BPC College ranging from November 1, 2012 to December 31, 2012. The log files are extracted and data pre-processing is done to eliminate the user requests since the focus is on the behavior of search engines. After extracting the two data sets, it is found that the data set 1 consists of 5,29,175 records for 8 weeks and data set 2 consists of 2,60,775 records. The entries with unsuccessful status code are eliminated.

The HTTP requests with POST and HEAD is also removed. In addition, all the user requests are removed to get the search engine requests. This is required as a user request in the input file may bias the results of search engine crawler behavior. After pre-processing the resultant file contained only the successful search engine crawler requests. [180Tanasa04] uses three heuristics to identify robots (crawlers).

1) Look for all hosts that have requested the page "robots.txt."
2) Use a list of user agents known as robots [202www.robotstxt.org/wc/robots.html.]

3) Compute the browsing speed. Browsing speed is computed as (Number of viewed pages)/(session time). If browsing speed exceeds a threshold θ_1 (pages/second), and the number of visited pages for that visit exceeds a threshold θ_2, it is considered to be a Web robot.

In our work some crawlers are identified from the IP address field. It contained substrings like "Googlebot", "Baiduspider", "MSNbot" etc. The user agents are also helpful in identifying the bots or crawlers like Ezooms, Discobot etc. The referrer URL containing "robots.txt" is also considered as the request from search engine crawlers.

5.4 Identification of Search Engine Crawlers and Visits

The tasks involved in identification of search engine crawler behavior are depicted in Fig. 5.1. Various search engine crawlers are identified from our data set. Certain search engine crawlers with number of visits less than 5 per week is removed as it is considered irrelevant. The bots Ahrefsbot, Seexie.com_bot, Turnitinbot, Yrspider are some of the bots in data set 1 whose number of visits are less than 5 in a week. For data set 2 the Alexa bot is considered irrelevant. The prominent crawlers identified and their description is listed in Table 5.1.

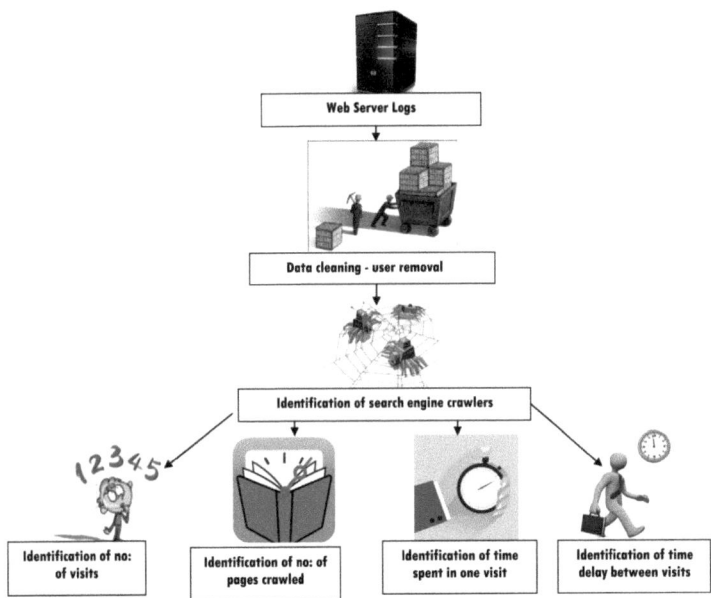

Fig. 5.1 Tasks involved in identification of search engine crawler behavior

Table 5.1 Prominent crawlers identified in each data set and their description

	Search Engine Crawler	Presence		Description
		Data set 1	Data set 2	
1	Ahrefsbot	N	Y	SEO spy crawler originating from Ukraine
2	Alexa	Y	N	Crawler from Alexa Internet, a subsidiary of Amazon.com
3	Baiduspider	Y	N	A Chinese search engine crawler
4	Bingbot	Y	Y	Crawler for Bing search engine
5	Discobot	Y	N	Experimental Web crawler for Discovery Engine
6	Exabot	Y	N	Bot from Exalead.com
7	Ezooms	Y	Y	Bot from Ezooms.com
8	Feedfetcher-Google	Y	N	Crawler from Google for RSS feeds
9	Googlebot	Y	Y	Main crawler from Google
10	Gosospider	Y	N	A Chinese search engine crawler
11	Ichiro	Y	N	Japanese Web spider sent by the search engine goo
12	Magpie	Y	N	A crawler from Brandwatch
13	MJ12bot	Y	N	Crawler from the UK based search engine Majestic-12
14	MSNbot	Y	N	Crawler developed by Microsoft for MSN search engine
15	Slurp	Y	N	A Web crawler from Yahoo
16	Sogou	Y	N	Crawler from the Chinese search engine Sogou
17	Sosospider	Y	N	Chinese crawler from Soso.com
18	SpBot	Y	N	A bot from OpenLinkProfiler.org
19	Yandex	Y	Y	A Russian search engine crawler
20	Yahoo	Y	N	A Web crawler from Yahoo
21	Yeti	Y	N	A crawler from Naver(Korean search engine)
22	Yodao	Y	N	A Chinese search engine crawler
23	Youdao	Y	N	A Chinese search engine crawler

The crawlers in data set 1 like Baiduspider, Discobot, Exabot, Feedtetcher-Google, Feedseeker, Gosospider, Ichiro, Magpie, MJ12bot, MSNbot, Seexie.com_bot, Slurp, Sogou, Sosospider, SpBot, Turnitinbot, Yahoo, Yeti, Yodao, Youdao and YrSpider are not present in data set 2. After pre-processing there are 22 crawlers for data set 1 and 5 crawlers for data set 2.

The crawler Alexa is an ethical robot which initially accesses the robots.txt file. It is a crawler from Alexa Internet, a subsidiary of amazon.com. The Alexa crawler identifies itself as ia_archiver in the HTTP "User-agent" header field. It uses a World Wide Web crawl strategy. Basically, it starts with a list of known URLs from across the entire internet, then it fetches local links found as it goes. There are several advantages to this approach, most importantly that it creates the least possible disruption to the sites being crawled [[191]http://www.alexa.com/help/Webmasters].

Baiduspider is the user agent of the search engine Baidu. It is a Chinese search engine crawler which crawls the server depending on the server load. Baidu has several user agents like Baiduspider for Web search, Baiduspider-mobile for mobile search, Baiduspider-image for image search, Baiduspider-video for video search, Baiduspider-news for news search, Baiduspider-favo for bookmark search and Baiduspider-ads for business search [[192]http://www.Webmasterworld.com/search_engine_spiders/4348357.htm].

Bingbot is the crawler for Bing search engine. It was developed by Microsoft. Earlier it was MSNbot which performed crawling activities for Bing but was replaced by Bingbot in 2010 [[193]http://user-agent-string.info/list-of-ua/bot-detail?bot=bingbot].

Discobot is the experimental Web crawler for Discovery Engine. They are still crawling, and their Website is still just an empty shell providing no information. A private alpha version of Discovery Engine became available in 2010. A beta version was released in 2011 [[194]http://whatis.riskyinternet.com/what-is/Web-robot/discoveryengine-robot-6142/].

Ezooms is a bot is from Ezooms.com which obtains content for unknown purpose. Ezooms uses the following user agent string EzoomsMozilla/5.0(compatible;Ezooms/1.0;ezooms.bot@gmail.com)[[195]http://www.rhyolite.com/anti-spam/badbots.html].

Feedfetcher-Google is a crawler from Google to keep up with new contents on the Web. Google collects atom feeds and RSS feeds when users choose to add them to their Google Homepage or Google Reader. Feedfetcher collects and periodically refresh these user-initiated feeds, but does not index them in Blog Search or Google's other search services [[196]http://support.google.com/Webmasters/bin/answer.py?hl=en&answer=1 78852].

Googlebot is a Web crawling spider from Google. Googlebot uses huge set of computers to crawl billions of pages on the Web. It uses an algorithmic process which involves computer programs to determine which sites to crawl, how often, and how many pages to fetch from each site. Googlebot's crawl process begins with a list of Webpage URLs, generated from previous crawl processes and augmented with sitemap data provided by Webmasters. As Googlebot visits each of these Websites it detects links SRC and HREF on each page and adds them to its list of pages to crawl. New sites, changes to existing sites and dead links are noted. This is used to update the Google index. Usually on an average Googlebot access the site not more than once every few seconds. However, due to network delays, it is possible that the rate will appear to be slightly higher over short periods. In general, Googlebot download only one copy of each page at a time. If Googlebot is downloading a page multiple times, it is probably because the crawler was stopped and restarted. Googlebot was designed to be distributed on several machines to improve performance and scale as the Web grows. To reduce the bandwidth usage, many crawlers on machines located near the sites are sent. Therefore, the logs may show visits from several machines at google.com, all with the user-agent Googlebot [[197]http://support.google.com/Webmasters/bin/answer.py?hl=en&answer=182072].

Ichiro is a Japanese Web spider sent by the search engine goo. MJ12bot is the search engine crawler from the UK based search engine Majestic-12. Majestic-12 operates a greatly enhanced crawl, with updates on its Web scale back links index on a daily basis. This back links index is open for queries using a dedicated, high performance search at MajesticSEO.com. Majestic-12 continues to offer Webmasters the ability to download data for their own sites for free via MajesticSEO and continues to invest in the improvement of its crawler and search infrastructure [[198]http://www.majestic12.co.uk/projects/ dsearch/].

Magpie is a robot used to obtain information from a specified list of Web pages for local indexing. It runs every two hours, and visits only a small number of sites [[203]http://www.robotstxt.org/db/magpie.html].

MSNbot is a crawler developed by Microsoft for MSN search engine. MSN search engine offers Webmasters the ability to slow down the crawl rate to accommodate Web server load issues. Websites that are small in terms of the number of pages and whose content is not regularly updated probably will never need to set crawl delay settings. The bot will automatically adjust its crawl rate to an appropriate level based on the content it finds with each pass. Larger sites that have a great many pages of content may need to be crawled more deeply and more often so that their latest content may be added into the index[[199] http://www.bing.com/blogs/site_blogs/b/Webmaster/archive/2009/08/10/crawl-delay-and-the-bing-crawler-msnbot.aspx].

Slurp is the Web crawler from Yahoo. The user agent for slurp is Mozilla/5.0 (compatible; Yahoo! Slurp;). The original developer of Slurp was Inktomi and later Yahoo acquired Inktomi [[200]http://help.yahoo.com/help/us/ysearch/slurp].

Sogou is the crawler from the Chinese search engine Sogou. It can search text, images, music and maps. Sosospider is a Chinese crawler from Soso.com. It is owned by Tencent Holdings Limited.

Yandex is a Russian search engine [[195]http://www.rhyolite.com/anti-spam/badbots.html]. The Ahrefsbot is a fast SEO spy crawler originating from Ukraine. These bots wastes the bandwidth and are banned by many Websites. The information collected by this bot is available for sale, provide opportunity for others to analyze one's content with the help of tools and also used for their own purpose also [201]http://blocklistpro.com/content-scrapers/ahrefsbot-seo-spybots.html].

The results for the number of visits made by various search engines of data set 1 is given in Table 5.2 and for data set 2 is given in Table 5.3. μ shows the mean number of visits for 8 weeks and σ shows the standard deviation of the visits of search engine crawlers.

Table 5.2 No: of visits by various crawlers for data set 1

No	Crawler	Week 1	2	3	4	5	6	7	8	Total	μ	σ
1	Alexa	1	5	10	1	2	0	2	3	24	3.00	3.2071
2	Baiduspider	128	222	65	89	124	67	66	47	808	101.00	56.866
3	Bingbot	157	166	159	175	126	100	118	96	1097	137.13	30.94
4	Discobot	113	33	0	21	24	52	5	69	317	39.63	37.424
5	Exabot	1	1	2	1	5	3	3	3	19	2.38	1.4079
6	Ezooms	50	48	40	22	0	23	38	41	262	32.75	16.74
7	Feedfetcher-Google	179	170	167	223	192	191	187	188	1497	187.13	17.283
8	Googlebot	211	226	238	273	212	207	200	207	1774	221.75	23.987
9	Gosospider	26	10	1	0	0	0	0	0	37	4.63	9.3034
10	Ichiro	117	81	122	146	0	42	21	33	562	70.25	53.803
11	Magpie	20	17	13	15	13	15	14	18	125	15.63	2.5036
12	MJ12bot	38	36	37	50	37	37	37	41	313	39.13	4.6426
13	MSNbot	24	17	11	19	15	12	18	15	131	16.38	4.1382
14	Slurp	149	114	144	190	144	145	160	145	1191	148.88	21.074
15	Sogou	48	34	37	54	40	44	43	60	360	45.00	8.7014
16	Sosospider	28	31	42	38	31	32	30	28	260	32.50	4.957
17	SpBot	3	3	3	4	2	2	1	1	19	2.38	1.0607
18	Yandex	51	71	57	72	102	44	51	74	522	65.25	18.638
19	Yahoo	22	0	0	0	0	1	1	0	24	3.00	7.6904
20	Yeti	3	4	1	4	3	2	4	4	25	3.13	1.126
21	Yodao	16	59	26	100	72	42	10	32	357	44.63	30.598
22	Youdao	2	4	1	1	18	1	3	0	30	3.75	5.8979

Table 5.3 No: of visits by various crawlers for data set 2

No	Crawlers	Week								Total	μ	σ
		1	2	3	4	5	6	7	8			
1	Ahrefsbot	79	0	1	19	37	66	31	48	281	35.125	28.59
2	Bingbot	31	41	27	43	23	30	28	17	240	30	8.635
3	Ezooms	3	20	26	38	26	24	9	28	174	21.75	11.09
4	Googlebot	42	49	42	44	42	49	35	60	363	45.375	7.405
5	Yandex	35	10	67	88	6	7	3	12	228	28.5	32.29

5.5 Identification of Pages Crawled

The number of pages crawled by various search engines is also analyzed to see the dynamic behavior of different search engines [231]Jose13]. Most of the search engines initially accessed the robots.txt file before crawling other pages except a few. Certain search engines crawled more pages compared with other crawlers. For example the crawlers like Googlebot, Slurp, Bingbot, Feedfetcher-Google, MJ12bot etc. crawled more number of pages and showed consistency in their behavior. Table 5.4 shows the number of pages crawled by various search engines for data set 1 and Table 5.5 shows the result for data set 2. μ shows the mean number of pages crawled for 8 weeks and σ shows the standard deviation of the number of pages crawled by search engine crawlers.

Table 5.4 No: of pages crawled by various crawlers for data set 1

No	Crawler	Week 1	2	3	4	5	6	7	8	Total	μ	σ
1	Alexa	2	13	27	2	4	0	4	4	56	7.00	8.96
2	Baiduspider	219	674	102	124	260	98	94	90	1661	207.63	199.03
3	Bingbot	368	559	519	526	404	232	287	647	3542	442.75	143.30
4	Discobot	889	161	0	119	92	289	6	178	1734	216.75	287.42
5	Exabot	2	11	4	2	11	6	5	6	47	5.88	3.52
6	Ezooms	235	160	77	57	65	59	83	67	803	100.38	63.79
7	Feedfetcher-Google	386	343	340	493	442	447	443	417	3311	413.88	53.81
8	Googlebot	841	895	682	847	655	525	540	556	5541	692.63	150.42
9	Gosospider	34	11	1	0	0	0	0	0	46	5.75	12.03
10	Ichiro	230	277	387	414	320	234	45	291	2198	274.75	113.86
11	Magpie	23	21	18	23	16	16	18	22	157	19.63	2.97
12	MJ12bot	174	304	224	392	255	285	294	316	2244	280.50	65.06
13	MSNbot	31	24	13	28	17	15	18	18	164	20.50	6.44
14	Slurp	367	253	297	410	310	264	308	331	2540	317.50	51.79
15	Sogou	72	42	47	61	52	54	51	80	459	57.38	12.89
16	Sosospider	32	38	57	42	36	36	35	33	309	38.63	8.03
17	SpBot	6	6	6	8	4	4	2	2	38	4.75	2.12
18	Yandex	140	250	99	171	216	102	212	276	1466	183.25	66.20
19	Yahoo	22	0	0	0	0	0	0	0	22	2.75	7.78
20	Yeti	6	9	2	7	7	4	7	7	49	6.13	2.17
21	Yodao	16	59	27	102	75	43	10	34	366	45.75	31.29
22	Youdao	4	8	2	2	25	2	7	2	52	6.50	7.86

Table 5.5 No: of pages crawled by various crawlers for data set 2

No	Crawler	Week								Total	μ	σ
		1	2	3	4	5	6	7	8			
1	Ahrefsbot	282	0	1	19	108	119	46	74	649	81.13	93.08
2	Bingbot	66	172	158	251	102	90	78	48	965	120.63	68.03
3	Ezooms	3	23	35	51	32	36	9	40	229	28.63	16.08
4	Googlebot	74	92	83	99	90	95	65	83	681	85.13	11.33
5	Yandex	39	18	123	199	6	7	4	13	409	51.13	71.65

5.5.1 Kruskal Wallis H Test

Kruskal Wallis H Test detects if n data groups belong or not to the same population [164Kruskal52] [136Paneerselvam04]. This statistic is a non parametric test suitable to distributions that are not normal such as the exponential distributions observed in Web Usage Mining or Web log analysis [100Ortega10]. The formula for H static of Kruskal Wallis test is given below where K is the number of samples.

$$H = \frac{12}{N(N+1)} \sum_{j=1}^{k} \frac{Rj2}{nj} - 3(N+1) \quad (5.1)$$

where Rj is the sum of the ranks of the sample j, nj is the size of the sample j, j=1, 2, 3, ...k and N is the size of the pooled sample $(n_1+n_2+........n_k)$. The calculated H value is to be compared against the chi-square value with (k-1) degrees of freedom at the given significance level α.

Case I

H_0: There is no significant difference between the number of visits made by various search engine crawlers.

H_1: There is significant difference between the number of visits made by various search engine crawlers.

Table 5.6 Test statistic for Case I

	Kruskall Wallis H Test	
	Data set 1	Data set 2
α	0.01	0.01
p-value	0.0001	0.044
Chi-square	148.734	9.799
df	21	4

From the test statistic in above Table 5.6, both the data sets showed a clear evidence of rejecting the null hypothesis. For data set 1, the p-value shows a strong evidence of rejecting the null hypothesis and for data set 2 shows a moderate evidence of rejecting the null hypothesis. The result of H test shows that there is a significant difference in the number of visits made by various search engine crawlers.

Case II

H_0: There is no significant difference between the number of pages crawled by various search engine crawlers.

H_1: There is significant difference between the number of pages crawled by various search engine crawlers.

The test statistic in Table 5.7 also showed that there is significant difference in the number of pages crawled by various search engines. The p-value for both the data sets is a strong evidence of rejecting the null hypothesis.

Table 5.7 Test statistic for Case II

Kruskall Wallis H Test		
	Data set 1	Data set 2
α	0.01	0.01
p-value	0.0001	0.013
Chi-square	154.85	12.714
df	21	4

A time series sequence plot is done for both the data sets with total number of visits and total number of pages crawled. The result for time series sequence plot for data set 1 is shown in Fig. 5.2 and for data set 2 is shown in Fig. 5.3. It is intended to see whether there exists any correlation between the number of visits and number of pages crawled. The Karl Pearson's Correlation Coefficient [136Paneerselvam04] is calculated for both data sets. The data set 1 showed a strong positive correlation of 0.932 whereas the data set 2 showed a moderate positive correlation of 0.505.

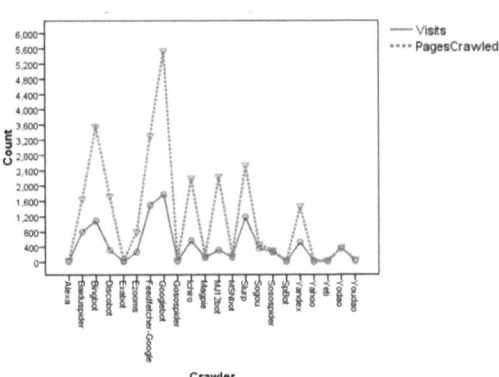

Fig. 5.2 Time series sequence plot for data set 1

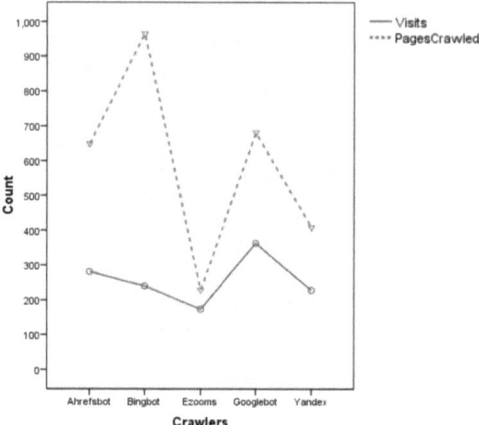

Fig. 5.3 Time series sequence plot for data set 2

5.6 Discovery of Temporal Behavior

The time spent by various crawlers is significant in identifying the server load as major proportion of the server load is constituted by search engine crawlers. A temporal analysis of the search engine crawlers is done to identify their behavior. It is found that there is a significant difference in the total time spent by various crawlers [232 Jose13]. The presence of search engine crawlers at Websites on hourly basis is also done to identify the dynamics of search engine crawlers at Websites. The log files of 2 different organizations are selected for study. The first data set is the log file of a business organization NeST of 30 days ranging from April 1, 2011 to April 30, 2011 and second data set belongs to an academic Website BPC College ranging from November 1, 2012 to November, 2012 comprising of 30 days. There are 17 distinct search engine crawlers for data set 1 and 5 distinct search engine crawlers for data set 2. Those search engines whose number of visits less than 5 in a month is eliminated before further analysis. It resulted in 14 search engine crawlers for data set 1 and

2 search engine crawlers for data set 2. Table 5.8 shows the results of pre-processing.

Certain search engine crawlers made several visits on one day itself whereas some others made one or two visits within a day. The time spent on a page is calculated by finding the difference between two consecutive requests. Table 5.9 and Table 5.10 shows total time spent in seconds by various search engine crawlers in data set 1 and data set 2 respectively. The prominent crawlers are Baiduspider, Bingbot, Discobot, Ezooms, Feedfetcher-Google, Googlebot, Gosospider, Ichiro, MJ12bot, MSNbot, Slurp, Sogou, Sosospider and Yandex. Some crawlers are not significant because they made less than 5 visits a month. It includes Alexa, Exabot, Magpie and Yrspider.

Table 5.8 Results of pre-processing

	Data set 1 April 1-30, 2011	Data set 2 November 1-30, 2012
Total number of records	2,65,476	1,45,680
Number of sucessful search engine requests	18,330	3,052
Number of distinct search engine crawlers	17	5
Number of search engine crawlers after pre-processing	14	2

Table 5.9 Total time spent in seconds by various search engine crawlers in data set 1

Day	Baiduspider	Bingbot	Discobot	Ezooms	Feedfetcher-Google	Googlebot	Gosospider	Ichiro	MJ12bot	MSNbot	Slurp	Sogou	Sosospider	Yandex
1	0	11760	0	0	17280	12900	960	8460	480	0	13920	5580	0	3420
2	4380	12420	36480	3540	7680	16860	780	28080	60	1680	16440	1140	0	3120
3	5880	13620	9600	3060	8460	35100	3360	12480	180	840	10140	1680	2760	1200
4	5880	6660	12120	3960	31140	20040	0	10200	120	120	10320	0	0	900
5	8580	11460	13020	3960	32160	46800	840	5700	180	0	19140	4260	0	1020
6	10620	24360	17100	4140	26760	37740	0	8520	60	60	13740	0	0	60
7	10620	24360	17100	4140	26760	37740	660	8520	1500	3780	13740	4620	1320	60
8	55680	24480	6900	4200	36000	23760	420	20760	60	0	9180	2280	0	2520
9	53880	28500	11040	6000	5760	46560	0	13560	300	60	10020	3000	0	6240
10	44880	19200	6480	2640	2760	10440	0	13320	180	0	0	0	1260	15000
11	54180	16800	8700	2580	24900	47340	0	0	180	0	9480	1800	0	12300
12	37200	13320	0	3900	30840	59340	0	17040	60	0	23700	1620	0	4500
13	29460	8760	2280	3180	26760	54780	1740	24480	1440	0	16320	0	0	3360
14	12660	10980	0	2520	20400	49980	1500	16140	180	3240	9360	360	5160	1080
15	2400	17160	0	1800	20280	30300	0	16800	240	180	14520	300	0	5760
16	1500	21000	0	1740	14160	27600	1680	46860	180	1440	17820	1800	660	60
17	2220	11820	0	1800	3780	34020	0	23520	120	0	12120	780	3600	1500
18	2940	22440	0	2460	26700	28740	0	5640	240	0	10140	0	0	6360
19	2760	18360	0	5700	26220	48240	0	4740	420	0	13200	600	2940	0
20	3120	13440	0	2280	27360	504600	0	27060	60	0	11460	120	900	0
21	120	8640	0	1140	32160	40980	0	20760	180	0	19140	2760	5700	2760
22	0	12000	0	1140	16320	13140	0	5040	1380	0	12660	1080	0	3600
23	1020	6480	0	1500	7860	46200	0	26040	1260	120	5880	0	0	0
24	2340	10320	0	1080	6300	43800	0	18060	300	60	7740	0	1320	1680
25	2040	12540	1860	1080	28680	28800	0	3360	300	60	11520	2220	0	3600
26	2220	18600	1920	2520	36960	14160	0	34440	240	0	14220	360	0	1800
27	3420	8340	1500	2340	36840	35460	0	7140	840	0	11580	0	1500	5100
28	420	4680	0	1380	35820	56400	0	17100	1800	0	13740	2460	0	300
29	2400	5640	0	540	42240	21360	0	41640	1620	0	13620	0	0	4380
30	0	11760	0	0	17280	12900	0	8460	1020	0	13920	660	0	1200

Table 5.10 Total time spent in seconds by various search engine crawlers in data set 2

Day	Bingbot	Googlebot	Day	Bingbot	Googlebot	Day	Bingbot	Googlebot
1	2040	3420	11	0	5520	21	0	3300
2	0	1740	12	0	2640	22	960	0
3	0	1620	13	0	2100	23	3240	11760
4	1620	4980	14	5760	4980	24	2220	2940
5	2340	4740	15	0	1740	25	0	5400
6	540	2640	16	1860	1020	26	11160	1140
7	2460	3000	17	10140	0	27	4380	900
8	3960	780	18	2940	6240	28	4560	1560
9	0	1500	19	0	3720	29	0	960
10	4020	2520	20	0	5460	30	0	3660

To analyze whether there is a significant difference in the total time spent, Kruskal Wallis H test described in Chapter 5.5.1 was used. The null hypothesis and alternate hypothesis are stated as follows.

H_0: There is no significant difference between the total time spent by various search engine crawlers.

H_1: There is significant difference between the total time spent by various search engine crawlers.

The test statistic for Kruskal Wallis H Test is shown in Table 5.11. For data set 1, the p-value shows a strong evidence of rejecting the null hypothesis and for data set 2 shows a moderate evidence of rejecting the null hypothesis. The result of H test shows that there is a significant difference in the total time spent by various search engine crawlers. The time distribution of various crawlers in data set 1 and data set 2 are analyzed for monitoring the presence of crawlers on an hourly basis in Websites. Fig. 5.4 to Fig. 5.17 shows the presence of prominent crawlers and their time distribution in data set 1.

Table 5.11 Test statistic

Kruskall Wallis H Test		
	Data set 1	Data set 2
α	0.01	0.01
p-value	0	0.026
Chi-square	285.655	4.963
df	13	1

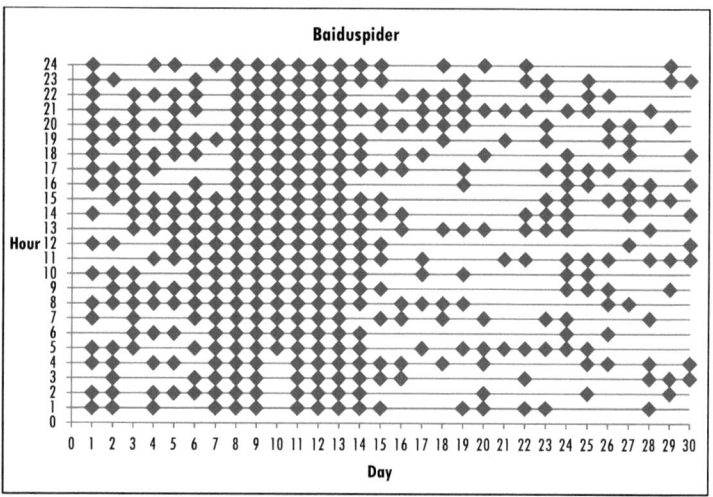

Fig. 5.4 Time distribution for Baiduspider in data set 1

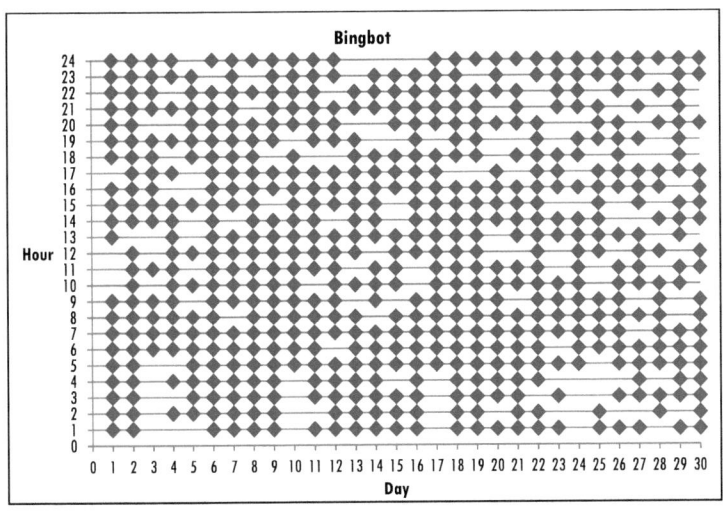

Fig. 5.5 Time distribution for Bingbot in data set 1

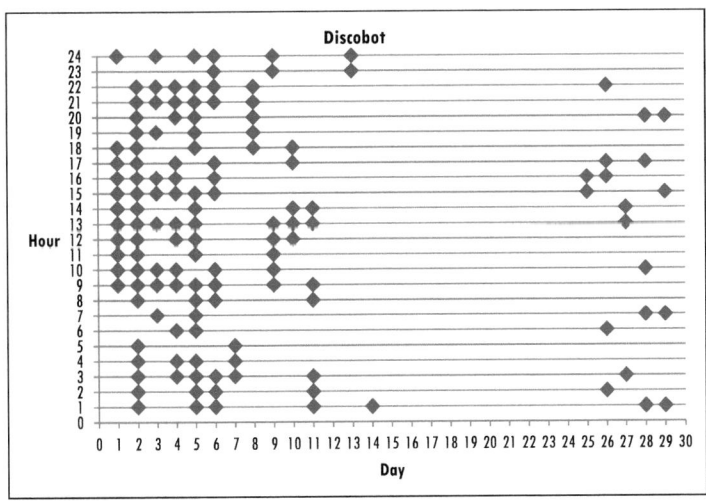

Fig. 5.6 Time distribution for Discobot in data set 1

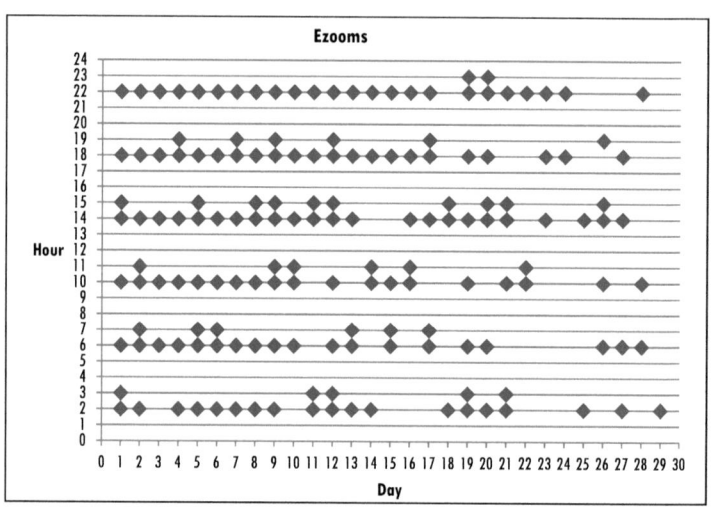

Fig. 5.7 Time distribution for Ezooms in data set 1

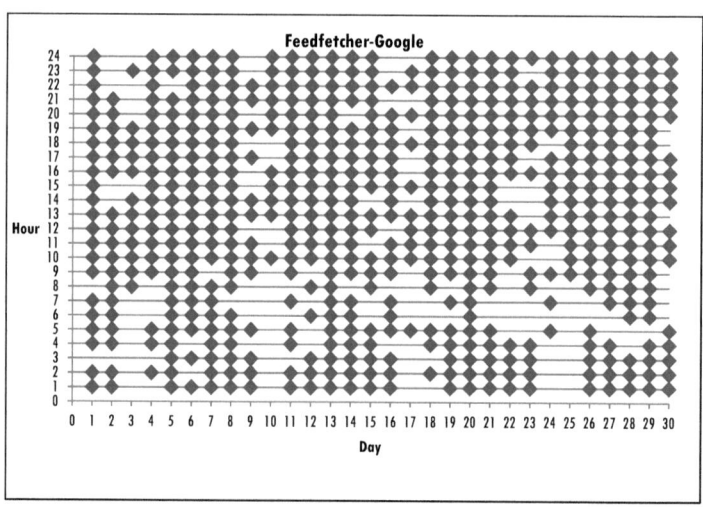

Fig. 5.8 Time distribution for Feedfetcher-Google in data set 1

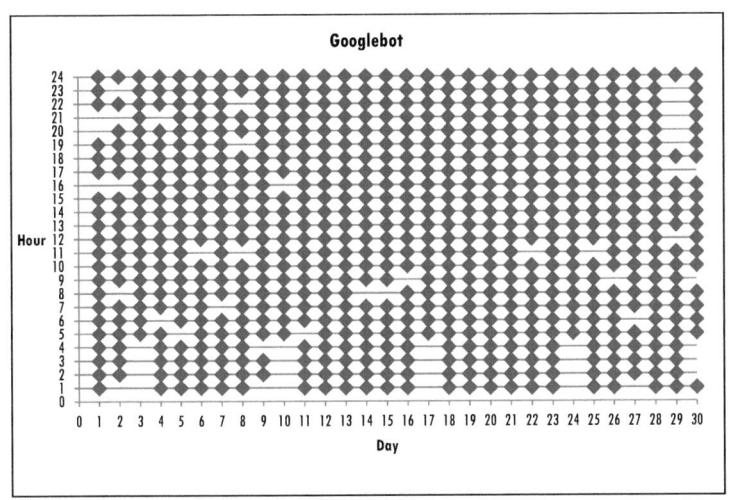

Fig. 5.9 Time distribution for Googlebot in data set 1

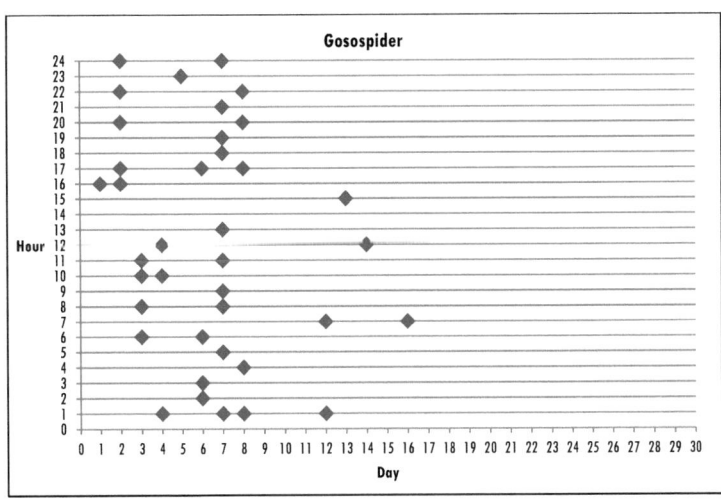

Fig. 5.10 Time distribution for Gosospider in data set 1

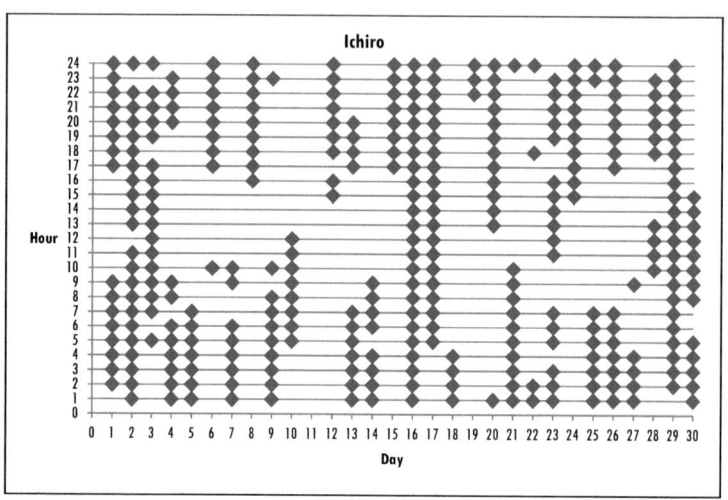

Fig. 5.11 Time distribution for Ichiro in data set 1

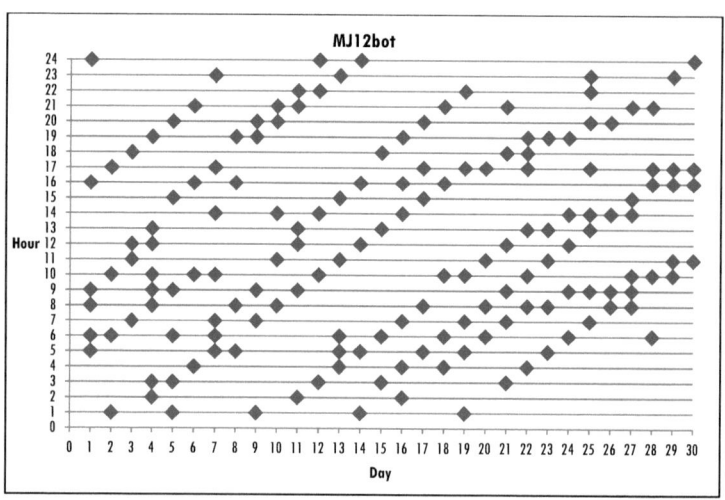

Fig. 5.12 Time distribution for MJ12bot in data set 1

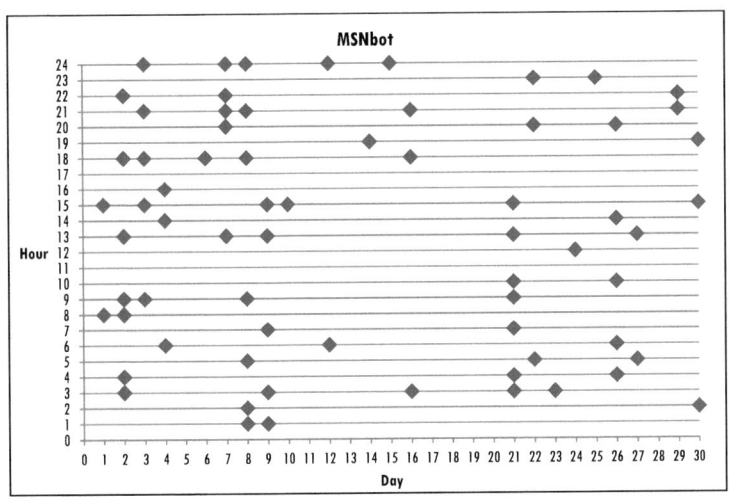

Fig. 5.13 Time distribution for MSNbot in data set 1

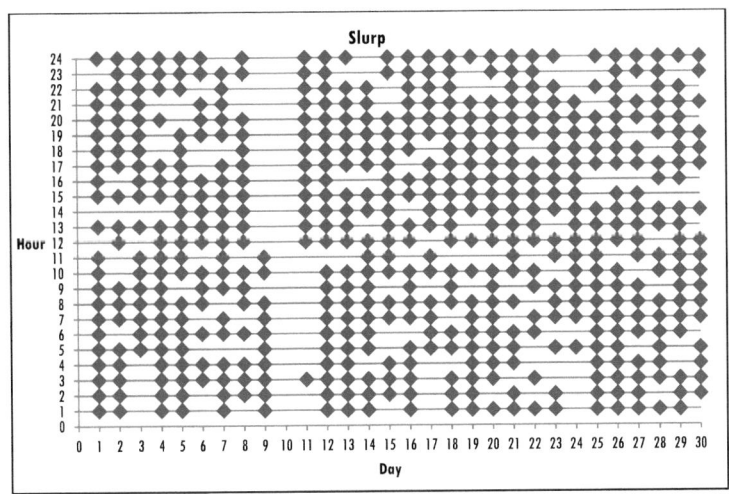

Fig. 5.14 Time distribution for Slurp in data set 1

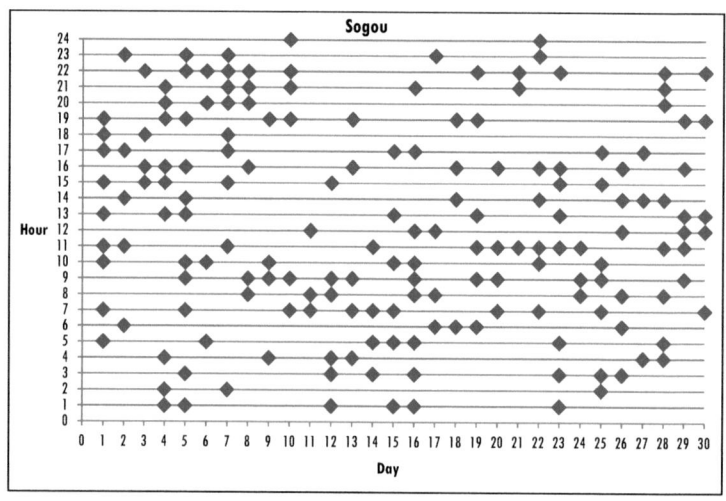

Fig. 5.15 Time distribution for Sogou in data set 1

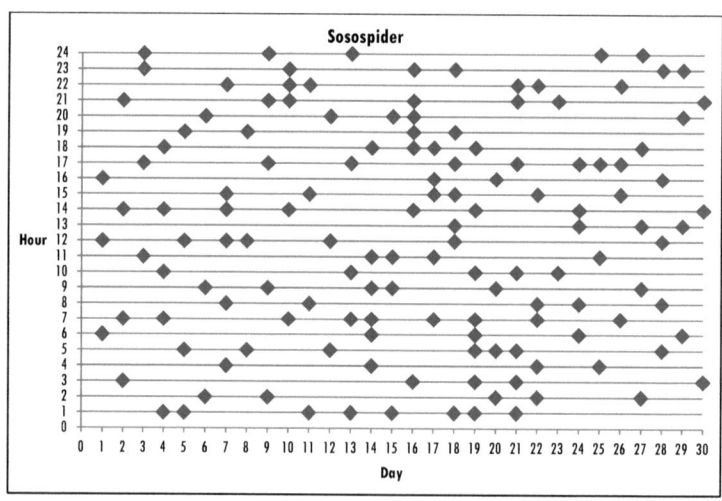

Fig. 5.16 Time distribution for Sosospider in data set 1

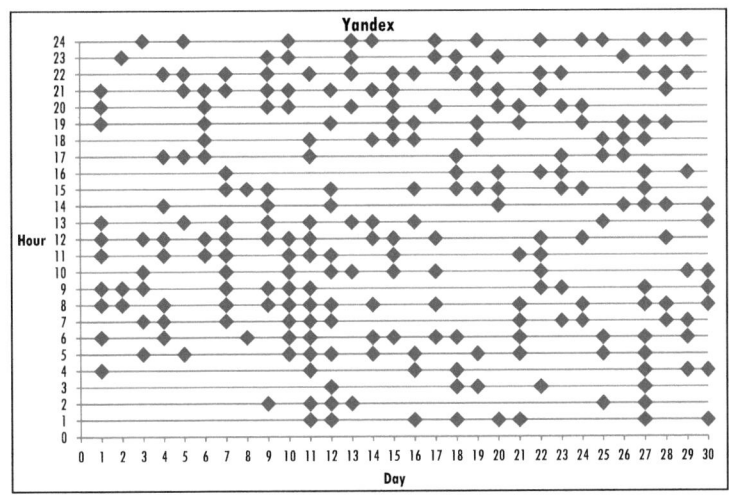

Fig. 5.17 Time distribution for Yandex in data set 1

Fig. 5.18 and Fig. 5.19 shows the time distribution of crawlers in data set 2.

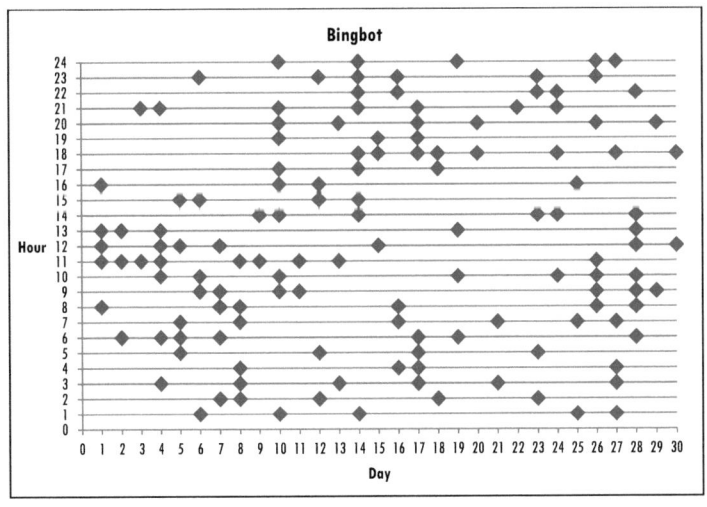

Fig. 5.18 Time distribution for Bingbot in data set 2

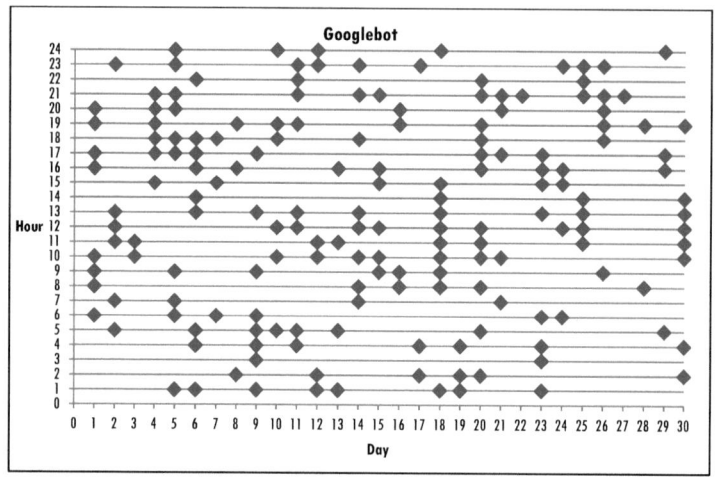

Fig. 5.19 Time distribution for Googlebot in data set 2

The results revealed that certain crawlers like Baiduspider, Bingbot, Feedfetcher-Google, Googlebot and Slurp are very dynamic crawlers and are present in almost every hour. Other crawlers like Discobot, Gosospider, MSNbot, Sogou, Sosospider etc. visited the Website with significant delay. They are less dynamic crawlers.

5.7 Discovery of Time Delay

The dynamicity of search engine crawlers could be identified with the time delay between two consecutive visits. The more the number of visits of a crawler to a Website, the more it contributes to the server load. It is analyzed to see whether there is a significant difference in the time delay between visits of a search engine crawler. Similarly the time delays between visits of various search engine crawlers are also analyzed to identify the differences in their behavior [230Jose13].

The Web log file of a business organization NeST ranging from May 1, 2011 to May 31, 2011 comprising of 31 days is selected for the analysis of time delay between the visits of a search engine crawler and among different search engine crawlers where the number of crawlers is significantly high. Table 5.12 shows the results of pre-processing. Those search engines whose number of visits is less than 5 in a month is eliminated before further analysis. There are 13 distinct search engine crawlers. Certain search engine crawlers made several visits on one day itself where as some others made one or two visits a day. The prominent crawlers are Baiduspider, Bingbot, Discobot, Ezooms, Feedfetcher-Google, Googlebot, Gosospider, Ichiro, MJ12bot, MSNbot, Slurp, Sogou, Sosospider and Yandex. Some crawlers are not significant because they made less than 5 visits a month. It includes Alexa, Exabot, Magpie and Yrspider.

Table 5.12 Results of pre-processing

	Data set 1 May 1-31, 2011
Total number of records	2,68,858
Number of sucessful search engine requests	21,230
Number of distinct search engine crawlers	17
Number of search engine crawlers after pre-processing	13
Number of visits chosen	100

5.7.1 Analysis of Variance (ANOVA)

Analysis of Variance (ANOVA) is used to analyze the variations in the collection of data among groups and within groups [136Paneerselvam04]. ANOVA conducted using a single factor is known as one way ANOVA [204http://www.stat.cmu.edu/~hseltman/309/Book/chapter7.pdf]. In this data set time delay in seconds for 100 visits (N=100) of 13 search engine crawlers are chosen for study. The single factor considered is the time elapsed between two consecutive visits of search engine crawlers. The following null hypothesis H_0 and alternate hypothesis H_1 is considered for ANOVA.

H_0: The means are equal.

H_1: The means are not equal.

Let k: the number of levels or groups in the experiment, N: total number of subjects in the experiment, n: number of subjects in each group, T: ΣX for each group, G: ΣX for the entire experiment, $\left(\sum T = G \right)$. Table 5.13 gives the formula summary for ANOVA.

Table 5.13 Formula Summary for ANOVA

Source	df	SS	MS	F	p
Between Groups	k-1	$\sum \dfrac{T^2}{n} - \dfrac{G^2}{N}$	$\dfrac{SS_{BG}}{df_{BG}}$	$\dfrac{MS_{BG}}{MS_{WG}}$	If P > 0.10 No evidence against the null hypothesis. If 0.05 < P < 0.10, Weak evidence against the null hypothesis. If 0.01 < P < 0.05 Moderate evidence against the null hypothesis. If 0.001 < P < 0.01 Strong evidence against the null hypothesis.
Within Groups	N-k	$\sum SS$ inside each group	$\dfrac{SS_{WG}}{df_{WG}}$		If P < 0.001 Very strong evidence against the null hypothesis.
Total	N-1	$\sum X^2 - \dfrac{G^2}{N}$			

The detailed statistic descriptive of the time delay in seconds between visits of search engine crawlers is given in Table 5.14 and results of One Way ANOVA is given in Table 5.15.

Table 5.14 Statistic descriptive of the time delay in seconds between visits of search engine crawlers in data set 1

Search Engine Crawlers	N	Mean	Standard Deviation	Standard Error	95% Confidence Interval for Mean		Minimum	Maximum
					Lower Bound	Upper Bound		
Baiduspider	100	4440.00	5620.870	562.087	3324.70	5555.30	900	29100
Bingbot	100	3886.80	2811.607	281.161	3328.92	4444.68	60	18540
Discobot	100	8052.60	24497.378	2449.738	3191.79	12913.41	120	146220
Ezooms	100	15196.80	11557.235	1155.723	12903.59	17490.01	1260	57600
Feedfetcher-Google	100	1957.20	3282.790	328.279	1305.82	2608.58	480	24060
Googlebot	100	1488.00	1112.573	111.257	1267.24	1708.76	180	6000
Ichiro	100	2387.40	9988.802	998.880	405.40	4369.40	180	94620
MJ12bot	100	15843.00	9565.892	956.589	13944.92	17741.08	2100	43080
Slurp	100	3662.40	2097.304	209.730	3246.25	4078.55	120	9900
Sogou	100	13288.80	10824.459	1082.446	11140.99	15436.61	540	45660
Sosospider	100	16754.40	9455.527	945.553	14878.22	18630.58	600	41040
Yandex	100	5429.40	4455.277	445.528	4545.38	6313.42	180	33600
Yodao	100	8065.80	2669.603	266.960	7536.09	8595.51	4500	21840
Total	1300	7727.12	11045.041	306.334	7126.16	8328.09	60	146220

Table 5.15 Results of One Way ANOVA

	Sum of Squares	df	Mean Square	F	Sig.
Between Groups	38239422380.308	12	3186618531.692	34.111	.000
Within Groups	120229399260.000	1287	93418336.643		
Total	158468821640.308	1299			

The significance is .000 and we reject the null hypothesis. Hence we conclude that there is a significant difference in the mean time delay. Fig. 5.20 shows the mean time plot of the time delay of various search engine crawlers in data set 1.

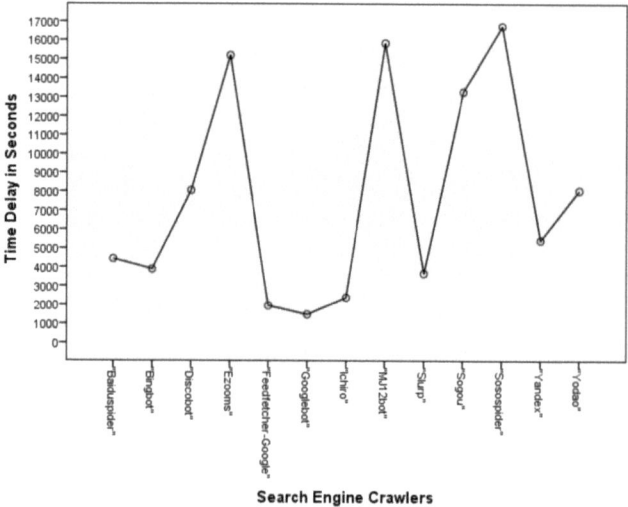

Fig. 5.20 Mean time plot of the time delay of various search engine crawlers in data set 1

5.7.2 Duncan's Multiple Range Test

Post hoc tests are used for situations in which the results have already obtained a significant omnibus F-test with a factor that consists of three or more means and additional exploration of the differences among means is needed to provide specific information on which means are significantly different from each other [205Duncan55]. Duncan's Multiple Range Test is a post hoc test. Table 5.16 shows the results of Duncan's Multiple Range Test. The significant difference or the range value is given by

$$R_p = r_{\alpha,p,v}\sqrt{MSE/n} \qquad (5.2)$$

where $r_{\alpha,p,v}$ is the *Duncan's Significant Range Value* with parameters alpha level $\alpha = \alpha_{\text{joint}}$, $p=$ range value and $v=$ MSE degrees of freedom. MSE is the mean square error from the ANOVA table and n is the number of observations used to calculate the means being compared.

Table 5.16 Results of Duncan's Multiple Range Test

Search Engine Crawlers	N	Subset for α = 0.05				
		1	2	3	4	5
Googlebot	100	1488.00				
Feedfetcher-Google	100	1957.20				
Ichiro	100	2387.40				
Slurp	100	3662.40	3662.40			
Bingbot	100	3886.80	3886.80			
Baiduspider	100	4440.00	4440.00			
Yandex	100		5429.40	5429.40		
Discobot	100			8052.60		
Yodao	100			8065.80		
Sogou	100				13288.80	
Ezooms	100				15196.80	15196.80
MJ12bot	100				15843.00	15843.00
Sosospider	100					16754.40
Sig.		.058	.244	.068	.077	.286

5.8 Conclusion

The obtained results for identifying the visits and pages crawled by various search engine crawlers point to the differences in the behavior of Web crawlers by various search engines. The more the number of search engine crawlers accessing a Website, the more will be its visibility when searching for a particular Website. The observed results showed that all search engine crawlers are not visiting all the Websites. In our experiment the data set 1 is accessed by more number of search engine crawlers compared to data set 2. Certain search engine crawlers are consistent in the number of visits and number of pages crawled while a few are not consistent or irregular in their visits and pages crawled. It is found that data set 1 is more visible to search engine crawlers as it is crawled by more number of search engine crawlers compared to data set 2. The results also showed a positive correlation between the number of visits and number of pages crawled. A better search engine optimization policy can be followed to make the Websites visible to different search engines so that the Websites will be listed top in the search engine rankings. A forecasting model could be developed in predicting the number of visits and number of pages crawled by different search engine crawlers.

The results of Kruskal Wallis H test for discovering the differences in total time spent by various crawlers showed that there is a significant difference in the behavior of search engine crawlers for both data sets. Certain crawlers like Googlebot, Feedfetcher-Google, Bingbot, Baiduspider etc. showed consistency in the time spent whereas certain other bots like Gosospider, MSNbot, Discobot etc. are not consistent in their behavior. The crawlers like Googlebot, Feedfetcher-Google, Bingbot and Baiduspider are dynamic and present in almost every hour which contributes a major portion of the server load.

The results of One Way ANOVA for analyzing the time delay between visits of search engine crawlers showed that there is a significant difference in the time delay between search engine crawlers and among repeated visits of the same crawler. The mean plot and Duncan's Multiple Range test revealed that the time delay of Googlebot, Feedfetcher-Google and Ichiro is almost similar. Similarly Slurp, Bingbot and Baiduspider showed a similar time delay which is higher than that of the first set of crawlers including Googlebot. All other crawlers showed significant time delay in visiting the Website. This shows that certain crawlers like Googlebot, Feedfetcher-Google, Ichiro, Slurp, Bingbot and Baiduspider are very dynamic compared to other crawlers like Ezooms, MJ12bot, Sosospider etc. Among the 13 crawlers, Googlebot showed least time delay for repeated visits and exhibited consistency in its behavior. The time delay can be further studied to develop a forecasting model for the time delay of search engine crawlers.

Two case studies using the data sets mentioned in Section 5.3 have been done to identify the presence of search engine crawlers both ethical and malicious in Web logs and the results are shown in Table 5.1. The results can be used to attain more visibility of the Websites to the crawlers by search engine optimization techniques which will increase the PageRank.

The results of these case studies have given information about the visit of spy crawlers also [[231]Jose13]. Based on this information, Website security measures can be developed and periodically measured.

A case study has been done on time distribution of 15 search engine crawlers. The results are plotted in graphs from Fig. 5.4 to Fig. 5.19. This shows how much each search engine crawler contributes to the server load [[230]Jose13][[232]Jose13]. Based on this search engine crawlers having high dynamicity can be regulated to crawl during off hours which will reduce the server load during peak hours.

5.9 Publications based on this Chapter

[1] Jeeva Jose, P. Sojan Lal, "Differences in Time Delay between Search Engine Crawlers at Web sites", *International Journal of Software and Web Sciences*, vol. 2, no. 5, 2013, pp.112-117. ISSN: 2279-0071

[2] Jeeva Jose, P. Sojan Lal, "Mining Web Logs to Identify Search Engine Behavior at Web sites", *Informatica*, vol. 37, no. 4, 2013, pp.381-386. ISSN: 1854-3871

[3] Jeeva Jose, P. Sojan Lal, "Analysis of the Temporal Behavior of Search Engine Crawlers at Web sites", *COMPUSOFT: International Journal of Advanced Computer Technology*, vol. 2, no. 6, 2013, pp.136-142. ISSN: 2320-0790

>> *End of Chapter 5* <<

Chapter 6: Forecasting of Search Engine Crawler Behavior

The number of visits and pages crawled by search engines could be helpful in identifying their behavior and also the server load. In the first section, a forecasting model in time series has been proposed for predicting the number of pages crawled by search engines. This model was compared with the actual values and it was found feasible. In the second section, the time delay between two consecutive visits of a crawler is predicted. The Auto Regressive Integrated Moving Average, ARIMA(1,1,0) Model in time series analysis works well with the forecasting of time delay between the visits of search engine crawlers at Websites. 5 search engine crawlers are considered, all of which could be modeled using ARIMA (1,1,0). The results of this study is useful in predicting the server load.

6.1 Background Literature

There are a few works in literature that describes about the temporal behavior of search engine crawlers. [206 Tripathy08] has proposed a Web Mining architectural model of distributed crawler for internet searches using PageRank algorithm and can run on a network of workstations. The crawler scales to several hundred pages per second, is resilient against system crashes and other events. They can be adapted to various crawling applications.

[207 Linda97] has made a study on the revisitation pattern of users on Web but had not mentioned about the revisitation patterns of search engine crawlers. Web revisitation patterns of users are examined by [208 Adar08]. The analysis revealed four primary revisitation patterns, each with unique behavioral, content and structural characteristics. They had illustrated how understanding revisitation patterns can enable Websites to provide improved navigation, Web browsers to predict user's destinations and search engines to better support fast, fresh and effective finding and re-finding. The temporal traffic patterns display strong regularities, with a large portion of future requests being statistically predictable by past ones.

Given the importance of topological measures such as PageRank in modeling user navigation, as well as their role in ranking sites for Web search [[209]Meiss08] had used the traffic data to validate the PageRank random surfing model. The ranking obtained by the actual frequency with which a site is visited by users differ significantly from that approximated by the uniform surfing/teleportation behavior modeled by PageRank. Time series analysis is a method often used to understand the underlying characteristics of temporal data in order to make forecasts.

[[210]Zhang09] has used a Web search engine transactional log and time series analysis to investigate user's actions. The analysis was conducted in two phases. In the initial phase, a basic analysis was employed and found that 10% of searchers clicked on sponsored links. In the second and more extensive phase, a one-step prediction time series analysis method along with a transfer function method was used. [[211]Olston08] had characterized the longevity of information found on the Web, via both empirical measurements and a generative model that coincides with these measurements. They had developed new recrawl scheduling policies that take longevity into account. Being the crawling policy of each search engine is usually commercial secret, it is useful to estimate each search engine's coverage and delay with known predicator variables.

[[212]Kim13] has proposed forecasting models for service coverage and delay of search engines in the Australian government area using predictor variables, identified from the crawling policies of academic papers and statistical regression methods. The Logistic regression method was employed for coverage forecast and Poisson regression method for delay. The search engines maintain the index of billions of pages for performing the search efficiently. To maintain the index of these search engines up-to-date, the crawlers of these search engines recursively retrieve the pages that cause 40% of current internet traffic and bandwidth consumption. These crawlers also cause load on the remote server by using its CPU cycles and Memory.

[215]Bal10] has addressed this problem by proposing a novel mobile crawling technique that uses mobile agents to crawl the pages. These mobile crawlers identify the modified pages at the remote site without downloading the pages. Therefore, only those pages are downloaded that are actually modified after the last crawl. This approach reduces the internet traffic and load on the remote site i.e. saves CPU cycles of the remote server. [216]Cho98] has studied in what order a crawler should visit the URLs it has seen, in order to obtain more "important" pages first. Obtaining important pages rapidly can be very useful when a crawler cannot visit the entire Web in a reasonable amount of time. Several importance metrics, ordering schemes and performance evaluation measures for this problem has been proposed. The results showed that a crawler with a good ordering scheme can obtain important pages significantly faster than one without. The working of a comprehensive full text search engine called WebCrawler was studied by [217]Pinkerton00]. [218]Koht-Arsa03] has done a study of high performance cluster based Web spiders. But there were no works in literature which predicts the number of pages crawled or forecasting models for predicting the time delay between two visits of a search engine crawler.

6.2 Forecasting of the Pages Crawled

Different search engine crawlers behave in different ways while they access a Website. A forecasting model in time series has been proposed for predicting the number of pages crawled by search engines. This model is compared with actual values and it is found feasible [233]Jose13]. The log files of 2 different organizations are selected for study. The first data set is the log file of a business organization

NeST of 45 days ranging from April 1, 2011 to May 15, 2011 and second data set belongs to an academic Website BPC College ranging from November 1, 2012 to December 15, 2012 comprising of 45 days. After extraction, there are 4,28,345 records for data set 1 and 2,38,446 records for data set 2. Pre-processing is done to eliminate unwanted and unsuccessful records. The successful search engine requests are filtered for further processing.

6.2.1 Forecasting Models

A forecast is an estimate of an event which will happen in future. The event may be the demand of a product or growth of a technology. The forecast value is not a deterministic quantity and only an estimate based on the past data related to a particular event. There are several forecasting techniques available. The shape of the curve representing the forecast of an event is one or more of the patterns given below [[140]Kothari04].

a) Horizontal pattern
b) Trend pattern
c) Seasonal pattern
d) Cyclic pattern
e) Random pattern

a) Horizontal pattern

A horizontal pattern exists when the data values fluctuate around a constant mean. Fig 6.1 shows a horizontal pattern.

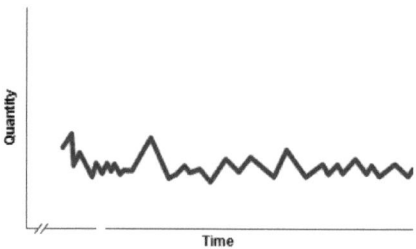

Fig. 6.1 Horizontal pattern

b) Trend pattern

In a trend pattern, data is progressively increasing or decreasing with time. Fig. 6.2 shows a trend pattern

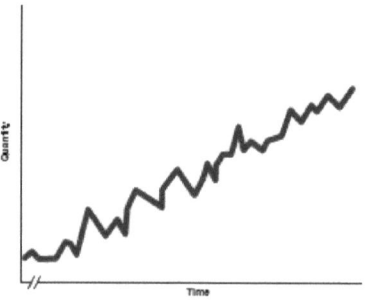

Fig. 6.2 Trend pattern

c) Seasonal pattern

The seasonal demand exists when the demand fluctuates according to some seasonal factors. Data exhibits a regularly repeating pattern at constant intervals. It may also directly linked with local/global economic factors. Fig. 6.3 shows the seasonal pattern.

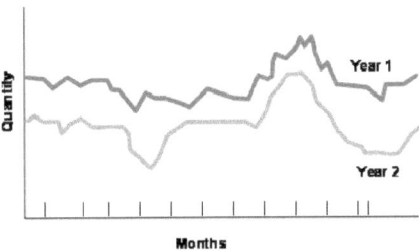

Fig. 6.3 Seasonal pattern

d) Cyclic pattern

The cyclic pattern shows the increase or decrease of data with time. Fig. 6.4 shows cyclic pattern.

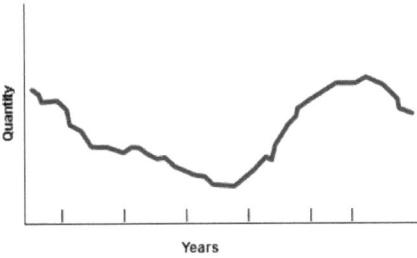

Fig. 6.4 Cyclic pattern

e) Random pattern

Random pattern may happen due to random process. This may exist in some situations for which no reason can be given.

6.2.2 Single Exponential Smoothing Method

The Web log data extracted from both data sets showed that the patterns for the number of pages crawled by various search engines exhibited random pattern. The data is also noisy and hence normalization is done before forecasting. There are several methods for normalization and the data is normalized using Min-Max normalization [220 Han12][221 Dunham03]. It is calculated as follows.

$$\text{À} = \frac{a - minA}{maxA - minA} (new_{maxA} - new_{minA}) + new_{minA} \qquad (6.1)$$

where minA = Minimum value from the observed values
maxA = Maximum value from the observed values
new_{maxA} = Maximum value for the new range
new_{minA} = Minimum value for the new range
a = value to be mapped
À = normalized value

The data values are mapped to a range [0, 1]. Single exponential smoothing method is a forecasting method used when the data shows a random pattern [136 Paneerselvam04]. There are double exponential and triple exponential smoothing methods available. Double exponential smoothing method is used whenever there is a trend in the data. Triple exponential smoothing method is used when there is seasonal changes as well as trend. Since both our data sets do not showed any trend, single exponential smoothing method is chosen. The forecast of the period t is computed by applying some correction over the forecast value of the immediate preceding period. The correction quantity is a portion α of the difference between the actual value of the immediate preceding period and the forecast of the immediate preceding period. The exponential smoothed forecast is computed as given below.

$$F_t = F_{t-1} + \alpha (D_{t-1} - F_{t-1}) \quad (6.2)$$

where F_t is the smoothed average forecast of the period t, F_{t-1} is the smoothed average forecast of the period (t-1), D_{t-1} is the actual value of the period (t-1) and α is the smoothing constant (0< α<1). Larger the α gives the more responsive forecast. It is taken α = 0.8 in this model which gave optimum values. For initial seed, the moving average of first two values is taken. The results of the normalization and exponential smoothed forecasts for both data sets 1 and 2 are given in Table 6.1. The Forecast Error (FE) is calculated as

$$FE = à - F_t \quad (6.3)$$

The Squared Forecast Error (SE) is calculated as

$$SE = (à - Ft)^2 \quad (6.4)$$

The Mean Forecast Error (MFE) is computed as

$$MFE = \sum_{t=1}^{N} \frac{(à - Ft)}{N} \quad (6.5)$$

The MFE for data set 1 is 0.02 and for data set 2 is 0.01. The Mean Squared Error (MSE) is calculated as follows.

$$MSE = \sum_{t=1}^{N} \frac{(à - Ft)2}{N} \quad (6.6)$$

The Mean Squared Error (MSE) for data set 1 is 0.04 and for data set 2 is 0.12. The actual forecasted value is calculated as

$$Ft' = \frac{à*(maxA - minA)}{(new_{maxA} - new_{minA})} - new_{minA} + minA \quad (6.7)$$

Fig. 6.5 and Fig. 6.6 show the graphical representation of observed values and forecasted values for the number of pages crawled at Website 1 and Website 2 respectively.

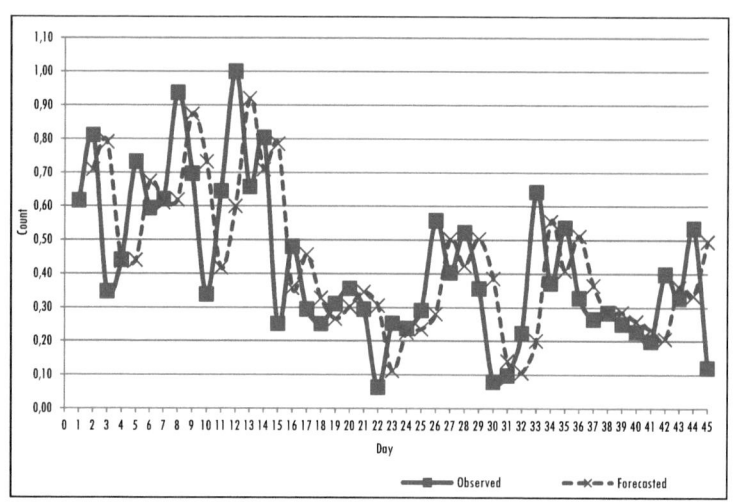

Fig. 6.5 Observed and forecasted values for the number of pages crawled at Website 1

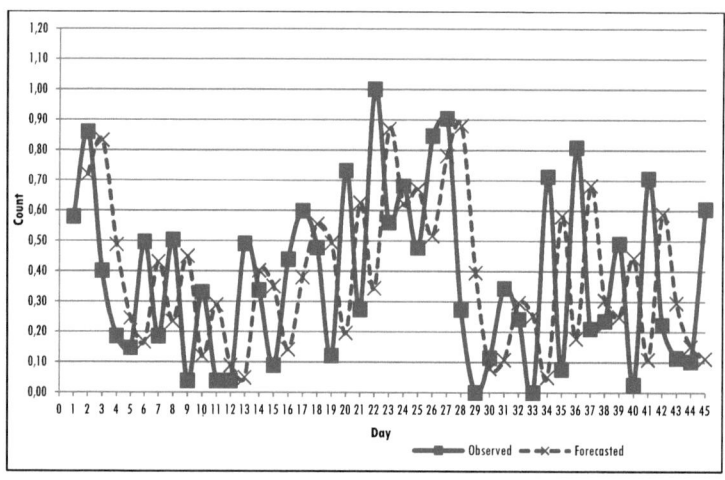

Fig. 6.6 Observed and forecasted values for the number of pages crawled at Website 2

Table 6.1 Results of normalization and exponential smoothed forecasts

	Data set 1						Data set 2					
Day (X)	Pages Crawled (Y)	à	F_t	FE	SE	F_t'	Day (X)	Pages Crawled (Y)	à	F_t	FE	SE	F_t'
1	611	0.62					1	101	0.58				
2	722	0.81	0.71	-0.10	0.01	664	2	145	0.86	0.72	-0.14	0.02	123
3	457	0.35	0.79	0.44	0.20	710	3	73	0.40	0.83	0.43	0.19	141
4	510	0.44	0.44	0.00	0.00	508	4	39	0.18	0.49	0.30	0.09	87
5	677	0.73	0.44	-0.29	0.09	510	5	33	0.15	0.25	0.10	0.01	49
6	598	0.59	0.67	0.08	0.01	644	6	88	0.50	0.17	-0.33	0.11	36
7	613	0.62	0.61	-0.01	0.00	607	7	39	0.18	0.43	0.25	0.06	78
8	794	0.94	0.62	-0.32	0.10	612	8	89	0.50	0.23	-0.27	0.07	47
9	657	0.70	0.87	0.18	0.03	758	9	16	0.04	0.45	0.41	0.17	81
10	452	0.34	0.73	0.39	0.15	677	10	62	0.33	0.12	-0.21	0.04	29
11	627	0.65	0.42	-0.23	0.05	497	11	16	0.04	0.29	0.25	0.06	55
12	830	1.00	0.60	-0.40	0.16	601	12	16	0.04	0.09	0.05	0.00	24
13	634	0.66	0.92	0.26	0.07	784	13	87	0.49	0.05	-0.44	0.20	18
14	718	0.80	0.71	-0.09	0.01	664	14	63	0.34	0.40	0.06	0.00	73
15	402	0.25	0.79	0.53	0.28	707	15	24	0.09	0.35	0.26	0.07	65
16	533	0.48	0.36	-0.12	0.01	463	16	79	0.44	0.14	-0.30	0.09	32
17	427	0.30	0.46	0.16	0.03	519	17	104	0.60	0.38	-0.22	0.05	70
18	402	0.25	0.33	0.08	0.01	445	18	85	0.48	0.55	0.08	0.01	97
19	436	0.31	0.27	-0.04	0.00	411	19	29	0.12	0.49	0.37	0.14	87
20	462	0.36	0.30	-0.05	0.00	431	20	125	0.73	0.20	-0.54	0.29	41
21	427	0.30	0.35	0.05	0.00	456	21	53	0.27	0.63	0.35	0.12	108
22	294	0.06	0.31	0.24	0.06	433	22	167	1.00	0.34	-0.66	0.43	64
23	403	0.25	0.11	-0.14	0.02	322	23	98	0.56	0.87	0.31	0.10	146
24	394	0.24	0.23	-0.01	0.00	387	24	117	0.60	0.62	-0.06	0.00	100
25	425	0.29	0.24	-0.06	0.00	393	25	85	0.48	0.67	0.19	0.04	115
26	577	0.56	0.28	-0.28	0.08	419	26	143	0.85	0.52	-0.33	0.11	91
27	489	0.40	0.50	0.10	0.01	545	27	152	0.90	0.78	-0.12	0.02	133
28	557	0.52	0.42	-0.10	0.01	500	28	53	0.27	0.88	0.61	0.37	148
29	462	0.36	0.50	0.15	0.02	546	29	10	0.00	0.40	0.40	0.16	72
30	303	0.08	0.39	0.31	0.09	479	30	28	0.11	0.08	-0.04	0.00	22
31	314	0.10	0.14	0.04	0.00	338	31	64	0.34	0.11	-0.24	0.06	27
32	386	0.22	0.11	-0.12	0.01	319	32	48	0.24	0.30	0.05	0.00	57
33	626	0.64	0.20	-0.44	0.20	373	33	10	0.00	0.25	0.25	0.06	50
34	471	0.37	0.55	0.18	0.03	575	34	122	0.71	0.05	-0.66	0.44	18
35	565	0.54	0.41	-0.13	0.02	492	35	22	0.08	0.58	0.50	0.25	101

36	446	0.33	0.51	0.18	0.03	550	36	137	0.81	0.18	-0.63	0.40	38
37	410	0.27	0.37	0.10	0.01	467	37	43	0.21	0.68	0.47	0.22	117
38	421	0.28	0.29	0.00	0.00	421	38	47	0.24	0.30	0.07	0.00	58
39	402	0.25	0.29	0.03	0.00	421	39	87	0.49	0.25	-0.24	0.06	49
40	388	0.23	0.26	0.03	0.00	406	40	14	0.03	0.44	0.42	0.17	79
41	372	0.20	0.23	0.03	0.00	392	41	121	0.71	0.11	-0.60	0.36	27
42	486	0.40	0.21	-0.19	0.04	376	42	45	0.22	0.59	0.36	0.13	102
43	446	0.33	0.36	0.03	0.00	464	43	28	0.11	0.30	0.18	0.03	56
44	564	0.53	0.33	-0.20	0.04	450	44	26	0.10	0.15	0.05	0.00	34
45	327	0.12	0.49	0.37	0.14	541	45	105	0.61	0.11	-0.49	0.24	28

6.3 Forecasting of Time Delay

The Web log file of a business organization NeST ranging from May 1, 2011 to May 31, 2011 comprising of 31 days is chosen. Table 5.12 shows the results of pre-processing. We have chosen 5 prominent crawlers from our data set for study. It includes Baiduspider, Bingbot, Googlebot, Feedfetcher-Google and Slurp. These crawlers are consistent in their visits and hence chosen for modeling.

6.3.1 Model Identification

Let $y_1, y_2, y_3 \ldots y_T$ represent a sample of T observations of a variable of interest y and $\{y_t\}$ represents the time series. Since the stationary property is essential for the identification of an Auto Regressive Integrated Moving Average (ARIMA) model, the first step is always to test for stationary property of the underlying series. Many data in real time including the Web data chosen for our study is not stationary. The series can be made stationary by differencing with or without pre-transformations. Formally, $\{y_t\}$ is said to be stationary if the mean, $E(y_t)=\mu$, the variance $Var(y_t)=E(y_t - \mu)^2$ and the covariance $Cov(y_t, y_{t-s})= E(y_t - \mu)(y_{t-s} - \mu)= \gamma_s$ are all stable over time. For the series to be stationary, it must not exhibit any stochastic trend (changing mean) or varying volatility (changing variance) [222Jaggia10] [227Zhang03].

The Box-Jenkins procedure is concerned with fitting an ARIMA model to data [223Box84]. It has three parts: identification, estimation and verification. Fig. 6.7 shows the Box-Jenkin's model building process. The Box-Jenkins approach suggests short and seasonal (long) differencing to achieve stationary in the mean and logarithmic or power transformation to achieve stationary property in the variance. In case the series are seasonal, the Box-Jenkins methodology proposes multiplicative seasonal models coupled with long-term differencing, if necessary, to achieve stationary property in the mean. The difficulty with such an approach is that there is practically never enough data available to determine the appropriate level of the seasonal ARMA model with any reasonable degree of confidence. Users therefore proceed through trial and error in both identifying an appropriate seasonal model and also in selecting the right long-term (seasonal) differencing. In addition, seasonality complicates the utilization of ARMA models as it requires using many more data while increasing the modeling options available and making the selection of an appropriate model more difficult [228Makridakis84].

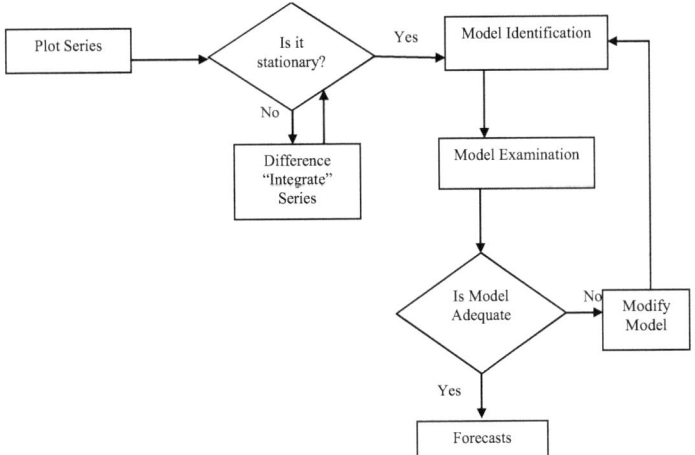

Fig. 6.7 Box-Jenkin's model building process

6.3.2 Autocorrelation Function (ACF) and Partial Autocorrelation Function (PACF)

The principal way to determine which Auto Regressive (AR) or Moving Average (MA) model is appropriate is to look at the Autocorrelation Function (ACF) and Partial Autocorrelation Function (PACF) of the time series. The plot of the autocorrelation function and partial autocorrelation function also serves as a visual test for stationary property [224 Weisang08] [225 Wei06]. At lag k, the ACF is computed by

$$ACF_{(k)} = \frac{E[(y_t - E[y_t])(y_{t-k} - E[y_{t-k}])]}{\sqrt{Var[y_t]\,Var[y_{t-k}]}} \qquad (6.8)$$

In time series, we may want to measure the relationship between y_t and y_{t-k} when the effects of other time lags 1, 2,...,k – 1 have been removed. The Autocorrelation does not measure this. However, Partial Autocorrelation is a way to measure this effect. The partial autocorrelation of a time series at lag k is denoted α_k and is found as follows

1) Fit a linear regression of y_t to the first k lags (i.e. fit an $AR_{(k)}$ model to the time series:

$$y_t = \varphi_0 + \varphi_1 y_{t-1} + \varphi_2 y_{t-2} + \cdots + \varphi_k y_{t-k} + \varsigma t.$$

2) Then $\alpha_k = \hat{\varphi}k$, the fitted value of φk from the regression (Least Squares). The set of partial autocorrelations at different lags is called the Partial Autocorrelation Function (PACF) and is plotted like the ACF.

100 time delay between consecutive visits for the crawlers Baiduspider, Bingbot, Googlebot, Feedtetcher-Google and Slurp are chosen. The time delay in seconds is plotted and Autocorrelation Function (ACF) and Partial Autocorrelation Function (PACF) are plotted. The obtained plot for Baiduspider is given in Fig. 6.8 and Fig. 6.9 respectively.

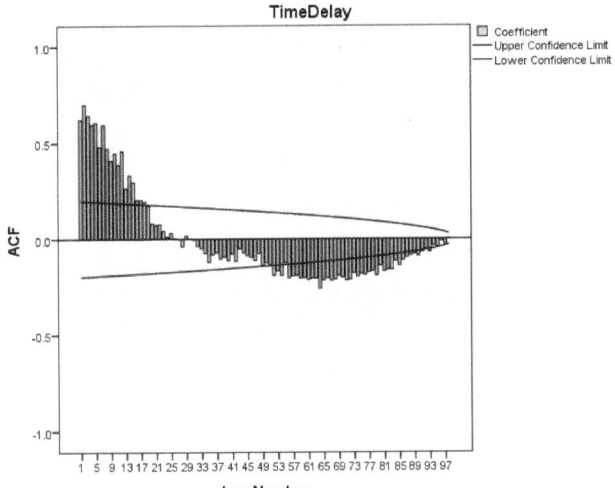

Fig. 6.8 ACF for Baiduspider

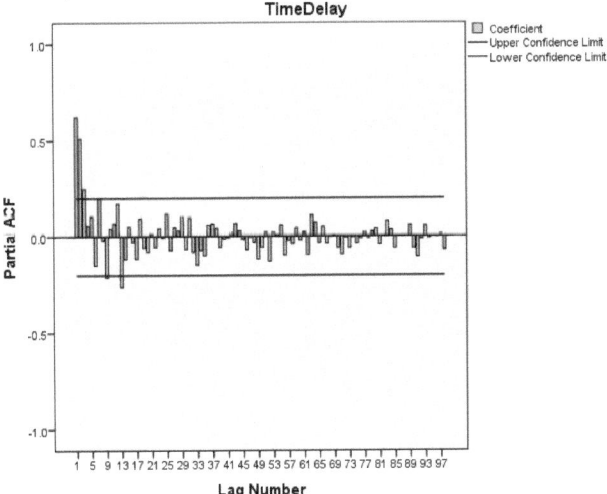

Fig. 6.9 PACF for Baiduspider

Similarly the Autocorrelation Function (ACF) and Partial Autocorrelation Function (PACF) plots of crawler Bingbot are shown in Fig. 6.10 and Fig. 6.11 respectively. The ACF and PACF plots of Feedfetcher-Google are shown in Fig. 6.12 and Fig. 6.13 respectively. Googlebot's ACF and PACF plot are plotted in Fig. 6.14 and 6.15 respectively. Fig. 6.16 and 6.17 respectively shows the ACF and PACF plot of Slurp. The ACF and PACF plots revealed that the data series could be modeled using Auto Regressive Integrated Moving Average Model ARIMA (1,1,0) the number of autoregressive terms and number of non seasonal differences as 1 and number of lagged forecast errors to 0 [[229]Jose13].

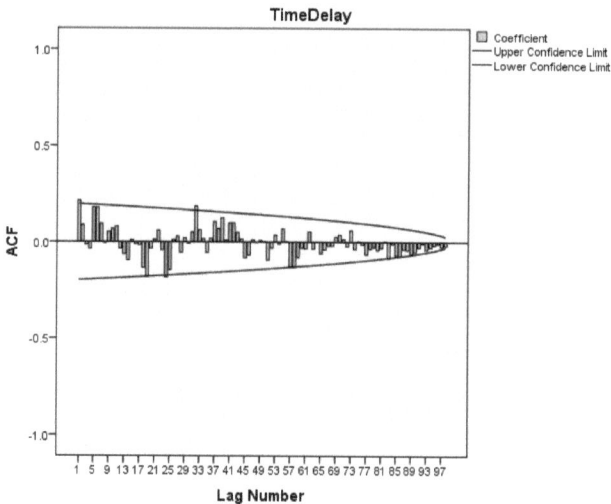

Fig. 6.10 ACF for Bingbot

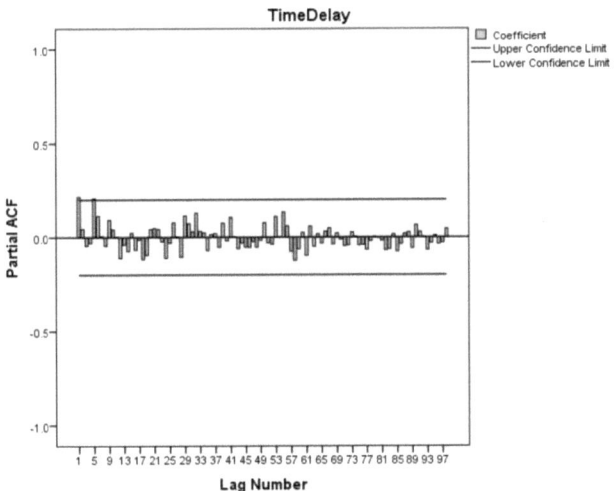

Fig. 6.11 PACF for Bingbot

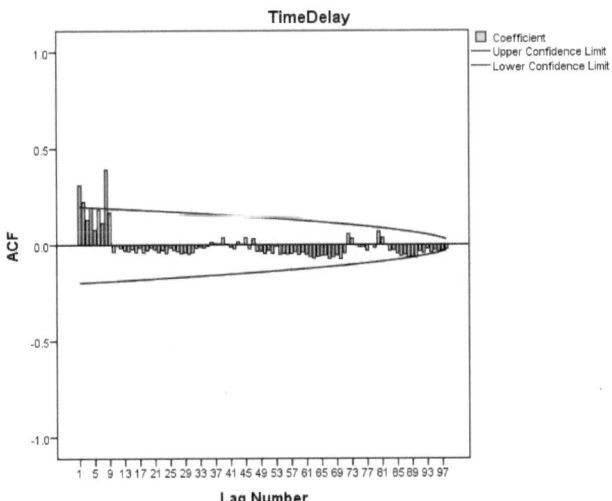

Fig. 6.12 ACF for Feedfetcher-Google

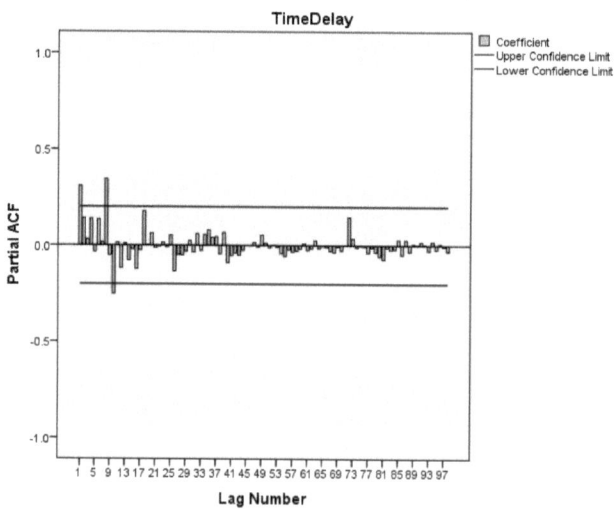

Fig. 6.13 PACF for Feedfetcher-Google

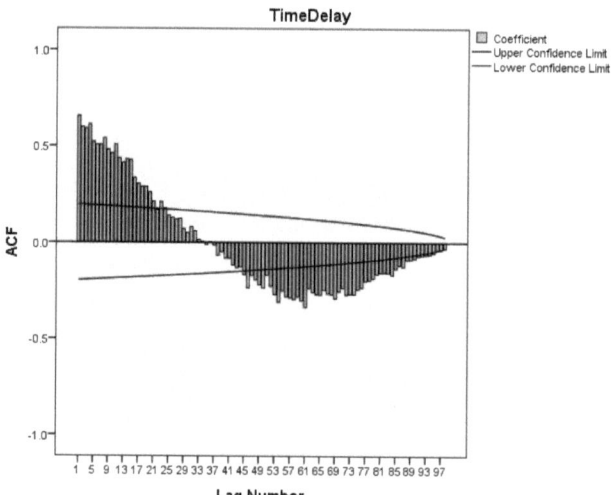

Fig. 6.14 ACF for Googlebot

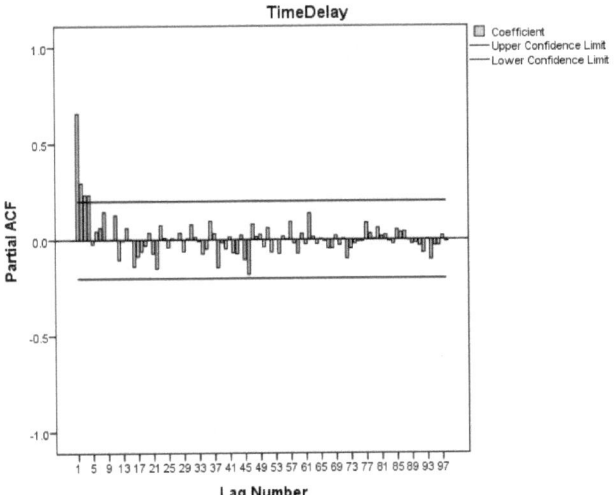

Fig. 6.15 PACF for Googlebot

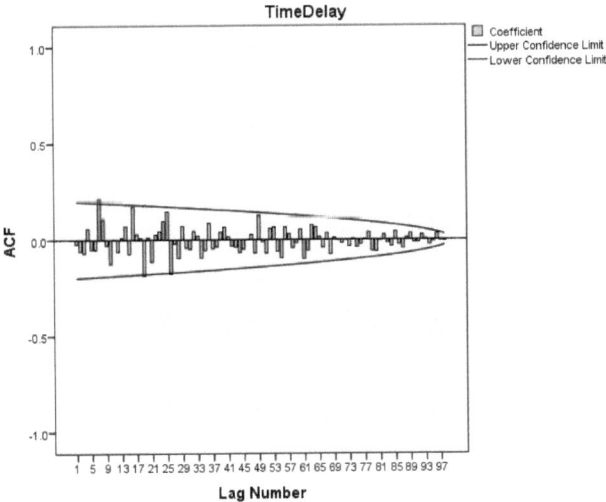

Fig. 6.16 ACF for Slurp

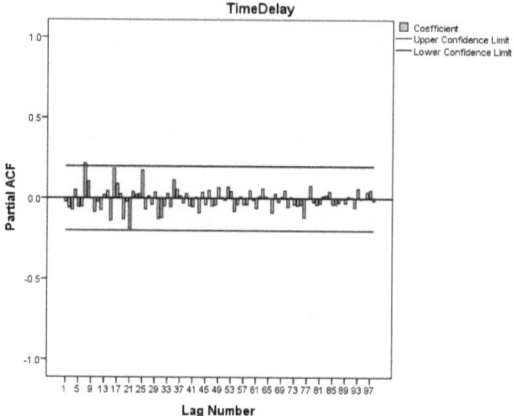

Fig. 6.17 PACF for Slurp

6.3.3 Auto Regressive Integrated Moving Average Model (ARIMA)

Forecasting is an important aspect of statistical analysis that provides guidance for decisions in all areas. It is important to be able to make sound forecasts for variables such as sales, production, inventory, interest rates, exchange rates, real and financial asset prices for both short and long term business planning. Autoregressive Integrated Moving Average (ARIMA) models provide a unifying framework for forecasting. These models are aided by the abundance of high quality data and easy estimation and evaluation by statistical packages [222 Jaggia10]. It was found that the time delay between the visits of search engine crawlers could be predicted using the ARIMA Model.

ARIMA (p,d,q): ARIMA models are, in theory, the most general class of models for forecasting a time series which can be made stationary by transformations such as differencing and logarithmic transformation. In fact, the easiest way to think of ARIMA models is as fine-tuned versions of random-walk and random-trend models. The fine-tuning consists of adding lags of the differenced series and/or lags of the forecast errors to the prediction equation, as needed to remove any last traces of autocorrelation from the forecast errors. Lags of the differenced series appearing in the forecasting equation are called "auto-regressive" terms, lags of the forecast errors are called "moving average" terms and a time series which needs to be differenced to be made stationary is said to be an "integrated" version of a stationary series [226Brockwell91]. Lag 1 is the time period between two observations y_t and y_{t-1}. Time series can also be lagged forward, y_t and y_{t+1}.

A non seasonal ARIMA model is classified as an ARIMA (p,d,q) model, where:

- p is the number of autoregressive terms,
- d is the number of non seasonal differences and
- q is the number of lagged forecast errors in the prediction equation.

The autoregressive element p represents the lingering effects of preceding scores, the integrated element d represents trends in the data and q represents the lingering effects of preceding random shocks. When the time series is long, there are also tendencies for measures to vary periodically called seasonality or periodicity in time series. Time series analysis is more appropriate for data with autocorrelation. If all patterns are accounted for in the model, the residuals are random. In many applications of the time series, identifying and modeling the patterns in the data are sufficient to produce an equation, which is then used to predict the future of the process.

ARIMA (1,1,0) is known as the differenced first order autoregressive model. It is represented by the equation

$$Y^{\wedge}(t) = \mu + Y(t-1) + \varphi(Y(t-1) - Y(t-2)) \qquad (6.9)$$

where μ represents the constant and φ is the autoregressive co-efficient.

The observed and forecasted values using ARIMA (1,1,0) of time delay between two consecutive visits of 5 crawlers namely Baiduspider, Bingbot, Feedfetcher-Google, Googlebot and Slurp are shown in Fig. 6.18, Fig. 6.19, Fig. 6.20, Fig. 6.21 and Fig. 6.22 respectively.

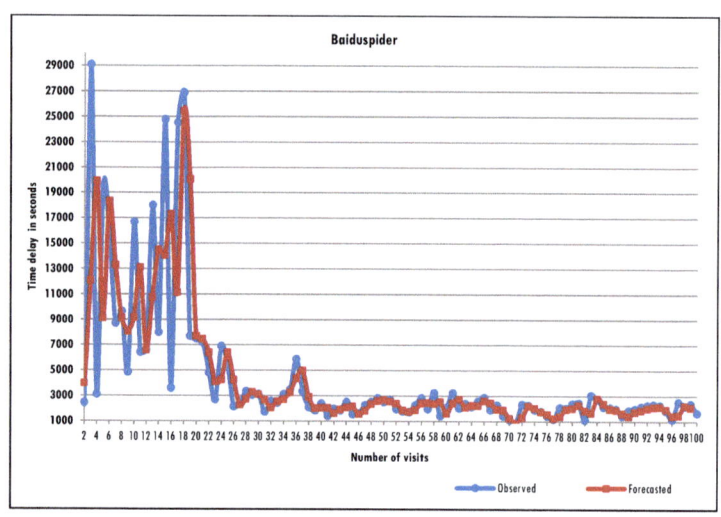

Fig. 6.18 Observed and forecasted values of time delay between two consecutive visits for Baiduspider

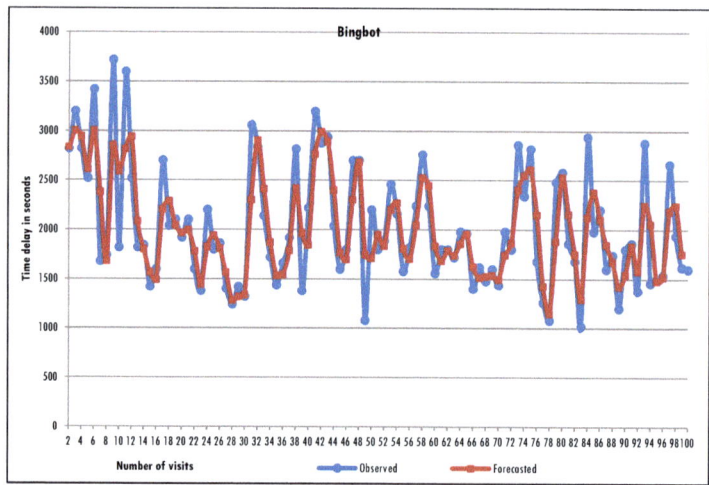

Fig. 6.19 Observed and forecasted values of time delay between two consecutive visits for Bingbot

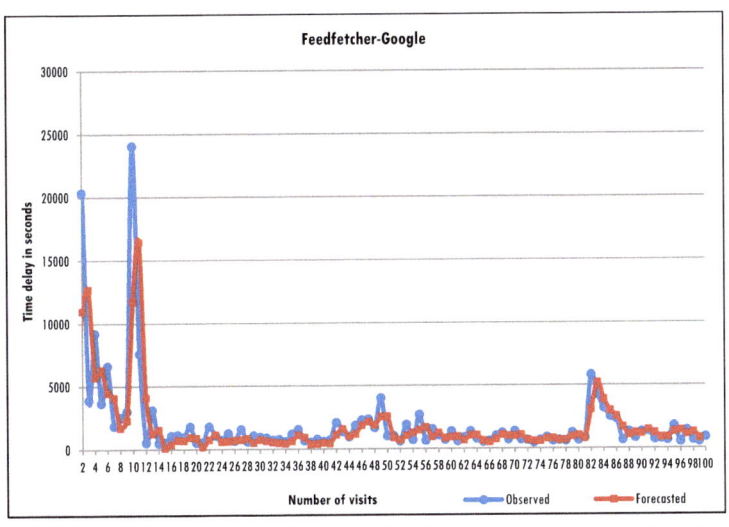

Fig. 6.20 Observed and forecasted values of time delay between two consecutive visits for Feedfetcher-Google

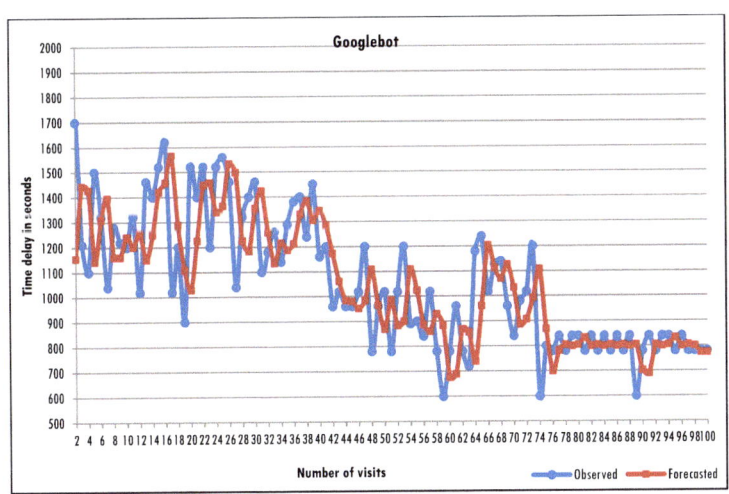

Fig. 6.21 Observed and forecasted values of time delay between two consecutive visits for Googlebot

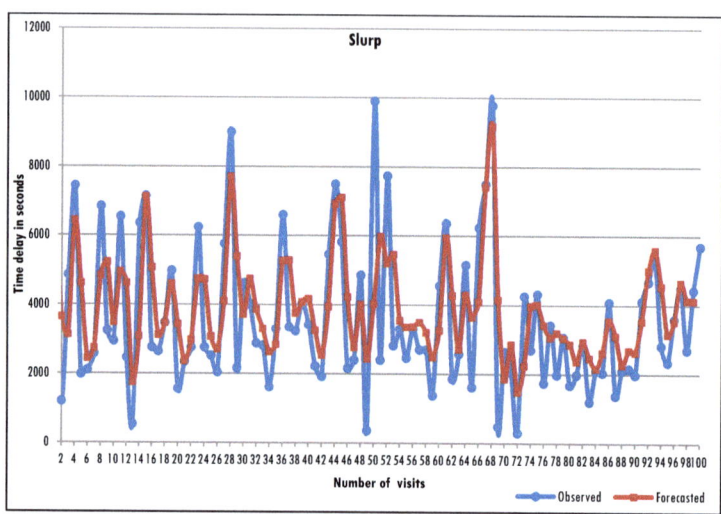

Fig. 6.22 Observed and forecasted values of time delay between two consecutive visits for Slurp

6.4 Conclusion

The results shown in Table 6.1 reveals that for both the data sets, the Single Exponential Smoothing method works well for forecasting the number of pages crawled at Websites. Since the data is noisy and does not showed any of the patterns, this model is well suited for making predictions for Web log data like the number of pages crawled at a Website. The Mean Square Error (MSE) and Mean Forecast Error (MFE) are very less for both the data sets which is an indication of the acceptance of this model.

The results of forecasting of time delay of search engine crawlers as given in section 6.3.3 reveals that Autoregressive Integrated Moving Average, ARIMA (1,1,0) model suits well for predicting the time delay between visits of search engine crawlers like Baiduspider, Bingbot, Feedfetcher-Google, Googlebot and Slurp. The Autocorrelation Function (ACF) and Partial

Autocorrelation Function suggested to opt for ARIMA (1,1,0) model. The crawlers like Baiduspider, Bingbot and Feedfetcher-Google showed more accuracy with this model than Googlebot and Slurp. This forecasting is helpful to calculate the server load and traffic. This work can be extended to find the time delay between two consecutive visits of crawlers on hourly basis to identify the crawlers visiting the Website during peak hours. The visits of such crawlers can be regulated and assigned to off hours so that the server load could be minimized.

6.5 Publications based on this Chapter

1. Jeeva Jose, P. Sojan Lal, "Application of ARIMA(1,1,0) for Predicting Time Delay of Search Engine Crawlers", *Informatica Economica*, vol. 17, no. 4, 2013, pp. 26-38. DOI: 10.12948/issn14531305/17.4.2013.03
2. Jeeva Jose, P. Sojan Lal, "A Forecasting Model for the Pages Crawled by Search Engine Crawlers at a Web Site", *International Journal of Computer Applications(IJCA)*, vol. 68, no. 13, 2013, pp.19-24. DOI: 10.5120/11639-7122

>> *End of Chapter 6* <<

Chapter 7: Conclusion and Scope for Future Work

7.1 Conclusion

The Web has revolutionized the conception of communication, interaction and information. The volume of Web data and its usage increases daily and this growth is not subject to any control. After the advent of data mining and its successful application on conventional data, Web usage data has been an appropriate and increasingly popular target of knowledge discovery. The introductory chapter gives an overview of different types of mining and particularly Web Usage Mining. The content of Web logs, which is the back bone of Web Usage Mining, is explained in detail in **Chapter 1**. The need for pre-processing and various pre-processing tasks gives an idea of the enormous size of the log file and the noise present in it. Web Usage Mining has a series of potential and diverse applications but are not limited to adaptive Websites, personalized recommendation, business intelligence, restructuring of complex Websites, mining association rules, sequential pattern mining, frequent sequential pattern mining, pre-fetching, caching and identification of search engine crawler behavior. Chapter 2, Chapter 3 and Chapter 4 analyzes user behavior while Chapter 5 and Chapter 6 identify the behavior of search engine crawlers that visits a Website.

Chapter 2 deals with pre-processing of Web logs and discovers the Web usage analytics. Indiscernibility relation in rough set theory is used for pre-processing of Web logs. Two algorithms are proposed for pre-processing of Web logs by constructing Equivalence Classes [[234]Jose2012][[240]Jose2012]. The first algorithm pre-processes the Web log for further identification of user behavior. These pre-processed Web logs are used for user and session identification. The second algorithm pre-processes the Web log for pre-fetching and caching. Two algorithms are proposed for usage analytics [235Jose2012] [238Jose2012]. The first one is for identifying the origin of visits, referring sites, the most popular keywords used to access the site and the second one extracts user agents which includes browsers and operating systems from the Web log.

Chapter 3 deals with clustering, an important data mining functionality. Though there were several works that mentions about clustering, there was hardly any work that mentions about the deep linking in a Website. An algorithm is proposed for clustering users based on *Entry Pages* [241Jose2012] to analyze the deep linked traffic which is crucial for E-commerce Websites. The percentage of traffic through Home page and other pages are obtained. This is repeatedly done for three months for data set 1 and two months for data set 2 to see the changes. Similarly a Rank Order Clustering algorithm is proposed for identifying similar user sessions from an *Entry Page* [237Jose2012]. The different sessions of *Top Ten Entry Pages* are given as input and the similar and dissimilar user sessions are obtained.

Chapter 4 deals with the sequence length and viewing time of users in a Website. Both the factors are considered as the two important characteristics of user behavior. The sequence length is important to identify potential users. Two cases are considered for analysis. The first case deals with the sequence length from the entry point. The mean sequence length of users entered from the Home page and other pages are tested using Two Sample Test for two data sets. It is found that the users entered through the Home page went deep into the Website than other users. The same is repeated for three months for data set 1 and two months for data set 2. It is observed that there is no change in the results for both data sets. The second case deals with the sequence length of repeated visits. The Two Sample Test is applied for users with single visit and users with repeated visits. The results showed that sequence length decreases in repeated visits. The same is repeatedly done for three months for data set 1 and two months for data set 2 to see the temporal change. But it is the same for both the data sets [239Jose2012].

Viewing time is considered as an important characteristic of user behavior. Based on the viewing time of various users on different pages, it can be classified as a content page or navigational page. The content pages are the potential pages on which users stay for a long time and are useful for E-commerce Websites for target advertising. A rough set approach is used for classifying content and navigational pages. The threshold is fixed based on percentile and pages in lower approximation are found to be content pages. The pages in upper approximation served as both content and navigational pages. Remaining pages are classified as purely navigational pages. This experiment is repeatedly done for two months in two different data sets and it is observed that the number and content pages varies with time [236Jose2013].

Chapter 5 discovers the various search engine crawlers accessing a Website. Two Web logs are chosen to identify the number of visits and pages crawled by various search engine crawlers. Kruskal Wallis H Test is used to see whether there is a significant difference in the behavior of search engine crawlers in terms of the number of visits and number of pages crawled [231Jose2013]. For both the cases and in both data sets, the results revealed that there is a significant difference in the behavior of search engine crawlers. The number of visits and number of pages crawled varied significantly from one crawler to another. Temporal behavior of search engine crawlers are also discovered [232Jose2013] to identify whether there is a significant difference in the amount of time spent by various crawlers. Kruskal Wallis H Test is applied to see the result.

Two data sets are used and the results of both the data sets revealed that there is a significant difference in the amount of time spent by various crawlers.

The time distribution of various search engine crawlers is plotted on an hourly basis to see the presence of various crawlers. The time delay between two consecutive visits of a crawler is studied [230Jose2013] to understand the dynamicity of search engine crawlers. ANOVA is used to identify whether there is a significant difference in the time delay between visits of same search engine crawler and among the search engine crawlers. The results revealed that there is significant difference in the time delay between and among crawlers. Duncan's Multiple Range Test is used to identify the search engine crawlers with similar or close time delay. Among the various crawlers, Googlebot is the most consistent and dynamic in its crawling behavior. Googlebot, Feedfetcher-Google and Ichiro showed almost similar time delay. Certain crawlers like Ezooms, MJ12bot, Sosospider are the least dynamic crawlers.

Chapter 6 proposes forecasting models for search engine crawler behavior. The first forecasting model is for predicting the number of pages crawled by a search engine crawler [233Jose2013]. A forecasting model based on single exponential smoothing method is used. This method is suitable when the data set shows random behavior. The Mean Square Error (MSE) and Mean Forecast Error (MFE) are very less which is an indicator for the acceptance of this model. The second forecasting model is to predict the time delay of various search engine crawlers [229Jose2013]. The Autocorrelation Function (ACF) and Partial Autocorrelation Function are plotted. The plots revealed that Auto Regressive Integrated Moving Average Model ARIMA(1,1,0) is suitable. The observed and forecasted values of five different search engine crawlers Baiduspider, Bingbot, Googlebot, Feedfetcher-Google and Slurp are plotted. The results showed that the forecasting models are acceptable.

7.2 Scope for Future Work

Now a days all governmental departments of our country have hosted Websites for providing information and the public is making use of it. Mining Web logs of these sites may give better insight about the user behavior at these sites. Market basket analysis can be done for commercial and trading Websites. In addition to this, travel and tourism, industry, education etc. is flourishing via Websites. Hence better performing Websites are inevitable. Information Communication Technology and E-governance is attaining rapid growth in our country. Our country has several Web portals for carrying out E-governance activities. Mining Web logs of these portals can discover better knowledge of the user behavior from these sites. This may lead to better design of these sites and provide better quality services to the clients. There are several future directions for extending the Web Usage Mining tasks.

As far as user behavior is concerned, several other Web Mining tasks can be initiated. Mining association rules, sequential pattern mining and frequent sequential pattern mining can be done based on the *Entry Pages* to identify the behavior of users entering through the same page. Similarly the reference length of the users based on *Entry Pages* and in repeated visits helps to identify the potential customers. Most of the works in Web Log Mining is in offline mode. A recommender system could be built by combining the data mining tasks and the Web logs in online mode. Since the size of the Web logs are very large, efficient methods need to be developed for storage and retrieval. Big data approaches can be used in Web Log Mining for efficient storage, retrieval and processing. There is the need of analyzing the log files for a longer period of one or two years to study the temporal and seasonal changes.

There are several studies that could be done with search engine crawlers. A separate study of ethical and unethical crawlers needs to be studied. The behavior of spy crawlers could be studied to understand their motives. The caching policy of various search engine crawlers could be studied to understand the dynamics of search engine crawlers.

>> End of Chapter 7<<

Acknowledgements

First and foremost I thank God Almighty who has showered his blessings throughout this research work.

I am deeply indebted to my guide Dr. P. Sojan Lal, Research Guide, School of Computer Sciences, Mahatma Gandhi University, Kottayam for his meticulous guidance, constant motivation and creative suggestions.

I acknowledge Kerala State Council for Science, Technology and Environment, Thiruvananthapuram for funding this research work.

My sincere gratitude to Ms. Bindhu V. R, Director, School of Computer Sciences, Mahatma Gandhi University, Kottayam for her co-operation and support. Special thanks to Dr. R. Vijayakumar, Former Director, School of Computer Sciences, Mahatma Gandhi University, Kottayam for the initiatives he has taken to conduct the coursework and for the encouragement through all the years of my research. I would also like to thank all the teaching and non-teaching staff at School of Computer Sciences for their co-operation.

I thank Dr. Sunny Kuriakose, Former Principal, Baselios Poulose II Catholicos College, Piravom for encouraging me to pursue research. I profusely thank all my colleagues at Baselios Poulose II Catholicos College, Piravom for their support and motivation.

My deepest gratitude goes to my family members for their unconditional support. Thanks to my husband Mr. Vijo Mathew for his support, persuasion and motivation for taking up the research. My two sons Samuel and Solomon deserves special thanks for the patience they have shown towards their mother to complete this research work. My heartfelt thanks go to my parents for their encouragement and support.

Finally I remember with gratitude all those who have rendered their help and assistance for this research.

Jeeva Jose

References

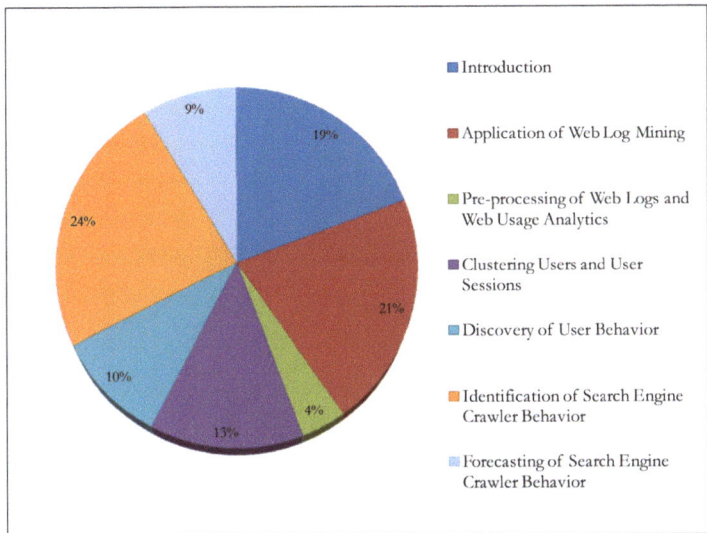

The references are segmented as Introduction, Application of Web Log Mining, Pre-processing of Web Logs & Web Usage Analytics, Clustering Users and User Sessions, Discovery of User Behavior, Identification of Search Engine Crawler Behavior and Forecasting of Search Engine Crawler Behavior.

[1] L. Liu *et al.*, "The Research of Web Mining", in *Proc. of the 4th World Congr. On Intelligent Control and Automation*, Shanghai, China, 2001, pp.2333-2337.

[2] R. Kosala and H. Blockeel, "Web Mining Research : A Survey", *SIGKDD Explorations Newslett.*, ACM, vol. 1, no. 1, pp. 1-15, 2001.

[3] M. F. Facca and P. L. Lanzi, "Mining interesting knowledge from Web logs: a survey", *Data & Knowledge Eng.*, vol. 53, pp.225-241, 2004.

[4] Q.Zhang and R. S. Segall, "Web Mining: A Survey Of Current Research, Techniques, And Software", *Int. J. of Inform.Technology & Decision Making*, World Scientific, vol. 7, no. 4, pp. 683–720, 2008.

[5] M. G. da Costa Jr. and Z. Gong, "Web Structure Mining : An Introduction", in *Proc. of the Int. Con. on Inform. Aquisition*, Hong Kong and Macau, China, 2005, IEEE, doi: [10.1109/ICIA.2005.1635156]

[6] R.Cooley *et al.*," Data Preparation for Mining World Wide Web Patterns", *Knowledge and Inform. Syst.*, vol. 1, no. 1, pp.5-32, 1999.

[7] W. Jicheng *et al.*, "Web Mining: Knowledge Discovery on the Web", in *Proc. of the IEEE Int. Conf. on Syst., Man and Cybern.*, Tokyo, 1999, vol.2, pp.137-141.

[8] A. Senthilkumar and N. Palanisamy, "Challenges for Web Mining", in *Proc. of the Int. Conf. on Computing, Commun. and Networking*, St. Thomas, VI , 2008, pp.1-6.

[9] H. Yu *et al.*,"Research Of Data Mining in Electronic Commerce", in *Proc. of the Int. Conf. on Consumer Electron., Communs and Networks*, XianNing, 2011, pp.4323-4326.

[10] S. K. Malik *et al.*,"Ontology and Web Usage Mining towards an Intelligent Web focusing Web logs", in *Proc of the Int. Conf. on Computational Intell. and Commun. Networks*, Bhopal, 2010, pp.443-448.

[11] J. Sivaramakrishnan and V. Balakrishnan,"Web Mining Functions in an Academic Search Application", *Informatica Economica*, vol. 13, no. 3, pp. 132-139, 2009.

[12] Y. Li *et al.*, "Research on Web Mining-Based Intelligent Search Engine", in *Proc. of the Int. Conf. on Machine Learning and Cybern.*, 2002, pp. 386-390.

[13] G. Lappas, "An overview of Web mining in societal benefit areas", *Online Information Review*, Emerald, vol. 32, no. 2, pp. 179-195, 2008.

[14] M.Grcar,"User Profiling: Web Usage Mining",in *Proc. of the 7th Int. Multiconf. On Info. Soc.*, Ljublijana,Slovenia, 2004.

[15] A. H. M.Wahab *et al.*," Data Pre-processing on Web Server Logs for Generalized Association Rules Mining Algorithm",*World Academy of Sci., Eng. and Technology*, pp.190-197, 2008.

[16] M. Spiliopoulou, "Web Usage Mining for Website Evaluation", *Commun. of the ACM*, vol. 43, no.8, pp.127-134, 2000.

[17] J. C. Bertot *et al.*,"Web Usage Statistics: Measurement Issues and Analytical Techniques", Government *Inform. Quarterly*, Jai Press Inc., vol. 14, no. 4, pp. 373-395, 1997.

[18] T.Hussain *et al.*, "Web Usage mining: A Survey on Preprocessing of Web Log File", in *Proc. of the Int. Conf. on Inform. and Emerging Technologies*, Karachi, 2010, pp.1-6.

[19] Z. Pabarskaite and A. Raudys, "A process of knowledge discovery from Web log data: Systematization and critical review", *J. of Intell. Inform. Syst.*, vol.28, pp. 79-104, 2007.

[20] Y. Woon et al., "Online and Incremental Mining of Separately-Grouped Web Access Logs", in *Proc. of the 3rd Int. Conf. on Web Inform. Syst. Eng.*, 2002, pp.53-62.

[21] T. T. Aye, "Web Log Cleaning for Mining of Web Usage Patterns", in *Proc. of the 3rd Int. Conf. on Comput. Research and Develop.*", Shanghai, 2011, pp.490-494.

[22] V. Ciesielski and A. Lalani, "Data Mining of Web Access Logs From an Academic Website", in *Proc. of the 3rd Int. Con. on Hybrid Intelligent Syst.*, 2003, pp.1034-1043.

[23] J. Lu et al., "Matrix Dimensionality Reduction for Mining Web Logs", in *Proc. of the IEEE/WIC Int. Conf. on Web Intell.*, 2003, pp. 405-408.

[24] K.P. Joshi et al., "On Using a Warehouse to Analyze Web Logs", *Distributed and Parallel Databases*, Kluwer Academic Publishers, vol. 13, pp. 161–180, 2003.

[25] S. Haigh and J. Megarity, "Measuring Website Usage: Log File Analysis", *Inform. Technology Services*, 1998, pp. 1-4, Available: https://www.ischool.utexas.edu/~i385df04/readings/Haigh-1998-Measuring_Web_Site_Usage.pdf.

[26] O. R. Zaiane, "Web Usage Mining for a Better Web-Based Learning Environment", in *Proc. of Conf. on Advanced Technology for Educ.*, 2001, Available: http://Webdocs.cs.ualberta.ca/~zaiane/postscript/CATE2001.pdf, Last retrieved October 2011.

[27] Internet: Hypertext Transfer Protocol Overview, Available: http://www.w3.org/protocols. Last retrieved October 2011.

[28] K. R. Suneetha and R. Krishnamoorthi, "Identifying User Behavior by Analyzing Web Server Access Log File", *Int. J. of Comput. Sci. and Network Security*, vol.9, no.4, pp.327-332, 2009.

[29] R. Kohavi, "Mining E-Commerce Data:The Good, the Bad, and the Ugly", *Advances in Knowledge Discovery and Data Mining*, LNCS, vol. 2035, pp. 2, 2001.

[30] D. Mican and D. Sitar-Taut," Preprocessing and Content/ Navigational Pages Identification as Premises for an Extended Web Usage Mining Model Development", *Informatica Economica*, vol. 13, no.4, pp.168-179, 2009.

[31] F. Zhang and H. Changc, "Research And Development In Web Usage Mining System--Key Issues And Proposed Solutions: A Survey", in *Proc. of the 1st Int. Conf. on Mach. Learning and Cybern.*, 2002, pp. 986-990.

[32] M.C.Burton and B. J.Walther, "A Survey of Web Log Data and Their Application in Use-Based Design", in *Proc. of the 34th Hawaii Int. Conf. on Syst. Sci.*, Maui, Hawaii, 2001, pp.1-10.

[33] J.Pitkow, "In Search of Reliable Usage Data on WWW", in *Proc. of the 6th Int. WWW Conf.*, Santa Clara, USA, 1997, pp. 1-14.

[34] L. Catledge and J. Pitkow," Characterizing Browsing Behaviors on the World Wide Web". *Computer Networks and ISDN Systems*, vol. 27, no. 6, 1995.

[35] J. Srivastava *et al.*, " Web Usage Mining : Discovery and Applications of Usage patterns from Web Data", *SIGKDD Explorations*, vol. 1 no. 2, pp.12-23, 2000.

[36] Q. Han *et al.*, "Study on Web Mining Algorithm Based on Usage Mining", in *Proc. of the 9th Int. Conf. on Comput.-Aided Industrial Design and Conceptual Design*, Kunming, 2008, pp.1121-1124.

[37] R.M. Suresh and R. Padmajavall,"An Overview of Data Preprocessing in Data and Web Usage Mining", in *Proc. of the 1st Int. Conf. on Digital Manage.*, Banglore, India, pp.193-198, 2006.

[38] S. R. Aghabozorgi and T. Y. Wah, "Recommender Systems: Incremental Clustering on Web Log Data", in *Proc. of the 2nd Int. Conf. on Interaction Sci.: Inform. Technology, Culture and Human*, Seoul, Korea, 2009, pp.812-818.

[39] G. T. Raju and P. S. Satyanarayana, "Knowledge Discovery from Web Usage Data: Complete Preprocessing Methodology", *Int. J. of Comput. Sci. and Network Security*, vol.8, no.1, pp. 179-186, 2008.

[40] S. Peng and Q. Cheng, "Research on Data Preprocessing process in the Web Log Mining", in *Proc. of the 1st Int. Conf. on Inform. Sci. and Eng.*, Nanjing, 2009, pp. 942-945.

[41] Y. Li et al., "The Construction of Transactions for Web Usage Mining", *in Proc. of the Int. Conf. on Computational Intell. and Natural Computing*, Wuhan, China, 2009, pp.121-124.

[42] S. B. Thakare and S. Z. Gawali," An Effective and Complete Preprocessing for Web Usage Mining", *Int. J. on Comput. Sci. and Eng.*, vol. 2, no. 3, pp.848-851, 2010.

[43] L. Zheng et al., "Optimized Data Preprocessing Technology for Web Log Mining", in *Proc. of the Int. Conf. on Comput. Design and Applicat.*, Qinhuangdao, 2010, pp. 19-22.

[44] M. Perkowitz and O. Etzioni, "Adaptive Websites", *Commun. of the ACM*, vol.43. no.8, pp.152-158, 2000.

45 J.Lee and W. Shiu, "An adaptive Website system to improve efficiency with Web mining techniques", *Advanced Eng. Informatics*, vol. 18, pp. 129–142, 2004.

46 J. Han and K. C. Chang, "Data Mining for Web Intelligence", *Comput.*, IEEE, vol.35, no. 11, pp.64-70, 2002.

47 B. Mobasher *et al.*,"Discovery and Evaluation of Aggregate Usage Profiles for Web Personalization", *Data Mining and Knowledge Discovery*, vol. 6, no. 1, pp. 61-82, 2002.

48 S. Puntheeranurak and H. Tsuji, "Mining Web logs for a Personalized Recommender System ", *in Proc of the 3rd Int. Conf. on Inform. Technology: Research and Educ.*, 2005, pp.445-448.

49 M. Eirinaki and M. Vazirgiannis, "Web Mining for Web Personalization", *ACM Trans. on Internet Technology*, vol. 3, no. 1, pp.1–27, 2003.

50 Y. H. Cho *et al.*," A personalized recommender system based on Web usage mining and decision tree induction", *Expert Syst. with Applicat.*, vol. 23, pp. 329–342, 2002.

51 S. Flesca *et al.*, "Mining User Preferences, Page Content and Usage to Personalize Website Navigation", *World Wide Web: Internet and Web Inform. Syst.*, vol.8, pp.317–345, 2005.

52 X. Zhang *et al.*, "Personalised online sales using Web usage data mining", *Comput. in Industry*, vol. 58, pp. 772–782, 2007.

53 J.Velasquez *et al.*, "Combining the Web content and usage mining to understand the visitor behavior in a Website", in *Proc. of the 3rd IEEE Int. Conf. on Data Mining*, 2003, pp. 669-672.

[54] I. Ting, "Web-mining applications in e-commerce and e-services", *Online Inform. Review*, vol. 32 no. 2, pp. 129-132, 2008.

[55] K. Lau *et al.*, "Mining the Web for business intelligence: Homepage analysis in the internet era", *J. of Database Marketing & Customer Strategy Manage.*, vol. 12, .no. 1, pp. 32-54, 2004.

[56] R. Bose, "Advanced analytics: opportunities and challenges", *Ind. Manage & Data Syst.*, vol. 109 no. 2, pp. 155-172, 2009.

[57] C. Zhang *et al.*, "The Application Research on Web Log Mining in E-Marketing", in *Proc. of the 2nd Int. Conf. on e-Bus. and Inform. Syst. Security*, Wuhan, China, 2010, pp.1-4.

[58] R. Lian, "The Construction of Personalized Web Page Recommendation System in E-commerce", in *Proc. of the Int. Conf. on Comput. Sci. and Service Syst.*, Nanjing, 2011, pp.2687-2690.

[59] G. Chengjian and H. Lucheng, "Web Mining in Technology Management", in *Proc. of the Int. Seminar on Bus. and Inform. Manage.*, Wuhan, 2008, pp. 88-91.

[60] J. Mena and R. Pettit, "Web-mining case study: An Internet radio Website", *Interactive Marketing*, Henry Stewart Publications, vol. 3, no. 1, pp.46-52, 2001.

[61] E. Chou, "Redesigning a Large and Complex Website: How to Begin and a Method for Success", *in Proc. of the 30th Annual ACM SIGUCCS on User Services*, USA, 2002, pp. 22-28.

[62] R. A. Ruddle, "How do people find information on a familiar Website?", in *Proc. of HCI 2009 – People and Comput. XXIII – Celebrating People and Technology*, UK, 2009, pp.262-268.

[63] L. Hasan and E. Abuelrub, "Assessing the quality of Websites", *Appl. Computing and Informatics*, vol. 9, pp. 11–29, 2011.

[64] Z. Jiang and S. Song, "Design and Implementation of Discovering Preferred Browsing Paths from Web Logs Algorithm", in *Proc. of the Int. Conf. on Educational and Inform. Technology*, Chongqing, China 2010, pp.415-418.

[65] H. Dai *et al.*, "Detecting Online Commercial Intention (OCI)", in *Proc. of the 15th Int. Conf. on WWW* Edinburgh, Scotland, 2006, pp. 829-837.

[66] Y. Yijun and C. Cun "Web User Log Mining For Web Retrieval", in *Proc. of the IEEE Region 10 Conf. on Comput., Commun., Power and Control Eng.*, 2002, pp.97-100.

[67] C. C. Yang *et al.*, "A Study on the User Navigation Path of a Web-based Intervention Program – AfterTheInjury.org", in *Proc. of the 1st ACM* Int. Health Informatics *Symp.*, Arlington, VA, USA, 2010, pp.449-453.

[68] J. Jose,"Web Mining and Challenges for Intellectual Property Protection", in *Proc. of the Int. Conf. on Inform. Soc.*, London, UK, 2010, pp.149-151.

[69] H. Liu and V. Keselj, "Combined mining of Web server logs and Web contents for classifying user navigation patterns and predicting users' future requests", *Data & Knowledge Eng.*, vol. 61, pp.304–330, 2007.

[70] X. Peng *et al.*, "Mining Web Access Log for the Personalization Recommendation", in *Proc. of the Int. Conf. on Multimedia and Inform. Technology*, Chiang Mai, Thailand, 2008, pp.172-175.

[71] M. Shyu *et al.*, "Mining user access patterns with traversal constraint for predicting Web page requests", *Knowledge and Inform. Syst.*, vol.10, no. 4, pp. 515–528, 2006.

[72] R. Agrawal and R. Srikant, "Fast Algorithms for Mining Association Rules", in *Proc. of the 20th VLDB Conf.*, Santiago, Chile, 1994, pp.487-499.

[73] J. W. Guan, D. A. Bell and D. Y. Liu, "The Rough Set Approach to Association Rule Mining", in *Proc. of the 3rd IEEE Int. Conf. on Data Mining*, 2003, pp. 529-532.

[74] X. Hu and N. Cercone, "Mining Knowledge Rules from Databases: A Rough Set Approach", in *Proc. of the 12th Int. Conf. on Data Eng.*, New Orleans, LA, 2006, pp.96-105.

[75] D. Liu *et al.*, "An Association Based Approach To Discovering Ordering Rules" in *Proc. of the 7th Int. Conf. on Mach. Learning and Cybern.*, Kunming, 2008, pp. 202-205.

[76] J. Han *et al.*, "Frequent pattern mining: current status and future Directions", *Data Mining and Knowledge Discovery*, vol. 15, pp. 55-86, 2007.

[77] S.Vijayalakshmi *et al.*, "Mining Constraint-based Multidimensional Frequent Sequential Pattern in Web Logs", *European J. of Scientific Research*, vol.36, no.3, pp 480-490, 2009.

[78] N. A. Sajid *et al*, "Sequential Pattern Finding: A Survey", in *Proc. of the Int. Conf. on Inform. and Emerging Technologies*, Karachi, Pakistan, 2010, pp. 1-6.

[79] H. Peng, "Discovery of Interesting Association Rules Based on Web Usage Mining", in *Proc. of the Int. Conf. on Multimedia Commun.*, Hong Kong, 2010, pp. 272-275.

[80] M. Nagi *et al.*, "Association Rules Mining Based Approach for Web Usage Mining", in *Proc. of the IEEE Int. Conf. on Inform. Reuse and Integration*, Las Vegas, USA, 2011, pp. 166-171.

[81] I.Tatarinov *et al.*, "Static Caching in Web Servers", in *Proc. of the 6th Int. Conf. on Comput. Commun. and Networks*, Las Vegas, NV,1997, pp.410-417.

[82] A. Iyengar *et al.*, "An Analysis of Web Server Performance", *Global Telecommun. Conf.*, Phoenix, AZ, 1997, pp. 1943-1947.

[83] F. Bonchi et al., "Data Mining for Intelligent Web Caching", in *Proc. of the Int. Conf. on Inform. Technology: Coding and Computing*, Las Vegas, NV, 2001, pp.599-603.

[84] F. Bonchi et al., "Web log Data warehousing and mining for intelligent Web caching", *Data & Knowledge Eng.*, vol. 13, pp. 165-189, 2001.

[85] Q. Yang and H. H. Zhang, "Web-Log Mining for Predictive Web Caching", *IEEE Trans. Knowl. Data Eng.*, vol. 15, no. 4, pp.1050-1053, 2003.

[86] Y. Huang and J. Hsu," Mining Web Logs to Improve Hit Ratios of Prefetching and Caching", in *Proc. of the IEEE/WIC/ACM Int. Conf. on Web Intell.*, 2005, pp. 577-580.

[87] J. Domenech et al., "Web prefetching performance metrics: A survey", *Performance Evaluation*, vol. 63, pp. 988–1004, 2006.

[88] A. Balamash et al., "Performance analysis of a client-side caching/prefetching system for Web traffic ", *Comput. Networks*, vol. 51, pp. 3673–3692, 2007.

[89] P. Gulati et al.,"A Novel Approach for Determining Next Page Access", in *Proc. of the 1st Int. Conf. on Emerging Trends in Eng. and Technology*, Nagpur, India, 2008, pp. 1109-1113.

[90] A. Songwattana, "Mining Web logs for Prediction in Prefetching and Caching", in *Proc. of the Int. Conf. on Convergence and Hybrid Inform. Technology*, Busan, 2008, pp.1006-1011.

[91] G. Pallis et al., "A clustering-based prefetching scheme on a Web cache environment", *Comput. and Elect. Eng.*, vol. 34, pp. 309–323, 2008.

[92] J. Domenech et al., "Using current Web page structure to improve prefetching performance", *Comput.. Networks*, vol. 54, pp. 1404–1417, 2010.

[93] S. Sulaiman *et al.*, "Intelligent Web Caching Using Adaptive RegressionTrees, Splines, Random Forests and Tree Net", in *Proc. of the 3rd Conf. on Data Mining and Optimization*, Putrajaya, Malaysia, 2011, pp. 108-114.

[94] H. H. Inbarani et al., "Rough set based Feature Selection for Web Usage Mining", in *Proc. of the Int. Conf. on Computational Intell. and Multimedia Applicat.*, Sivakasi, India,2007, pp.33-38.

[95] S. Hirano & S. Tsumoto, "An Indiscernibility Based Clustering Method", in *Proc of the IEEE Int. Conf. on Granular Computing*, Izumo, Japan, 2005, pp. 468-473.

[96] Z. Pawlak,"Rough Set Theory and its Applications", *J. of Telecommun. and Inform. Technology*, vol. 3, 2002,pp.7-10.

[97] Z. Pawlak & A. Skowron, "Rudiments of Rough Sets", *Inform. Sci.*, vol. 177, no.1, pp.3-27, 2007.

[98] Q. Yang et al., "Mining Web Logs for Prediction Models in WWW Caching and Prefetching", in *Proc. of the 7th ACM SIGKDD Int. Conf. on Knowledge Discovery in Databases*, San Fransisco, 2001,pp. 473-478.

[99] F. Hadzicand and M. Hecker, "Alternative Approach to Tree-Structured Web Log Representation and Mining", in *Proc. of the IEEE/WIC/ACM Int. Conf. on Web Intell. and Intelligent Agent Technology*, Lyon, 2011, pp.235-242.

[100] J.L. Ortega and I. Aguillo, "Differences between Web sessions according to the origin of their visits", *J. of Informetrics*, vol. 4, no.1, pp.331-337, 2010.

[101] Kohavi, R., and Parekh, R., "Ten Supplementary Analyses to improve E-commerce Websites", in *Proc. of the 5th Web Knowledge Discovery in Databases Workshop*, 2003.

[102] R. Baeza-Yates *et al.*, "Modeling User Search Behavior", *in Proc. of the 3rd Latin American Web Congr.*, 2005.

[103] R. A. Spinello, "An Ethical Evaluation in Website Linking", *ACM SIGCAS Comput. and Soc.*, vol. 30, no.4, pp. 25-32, 2000.

[104] R. Cooley *et al.*,"Web Mining: Information and Pattern Discovery on the World Wide Web", in *Proc. of the 9th IEEE Int. Conf. on Tools with Artificial Intell.*, Newport Beach, CA, 1997, pp.558-567.

[105] A.K. Jain *et al.*, Data Clustering: A Review", *ACM Computing Surveys*, vol. 31, no. 3, pp. 264-323, 1999.

[106] Y. Fu *et al.*, "Clustering of Web Users based on Access Patterns", in *Proc. of the 1999 KDD Workshop on Web Mining*, San Diego, CA, USA, 1999.

[107] J. Xiao and Y. Zhang, "Clustering of Web Users Using Session-based Similarity Measures", in *Proc. of the Int. Conf. on Comput. Networks and Mobile Computing*, Los Alamitos, CA, 2001, pp. 223-228.

[108] B.Hay *et al.*, "Clustering navigation patterns on a Website using a Sequence Alignment Method", in *Proc. of the 17th Int. Joint Conf. on Artificial Intell.*, Seattle, USA, 2001.

[109] D. He *et al.*, "Combining evidence for automatic Web session identification", *Inform. Process. and Manage.*, vol. 38, pp. 727–742, 2002.

[110] W. Wang and O. R. Zaiane, "Clustering Web Sessions by Sequence Alignment", in *Proc. of the 13th Int. Workshop on Database and Expert Syst. Applicat.*, 2002, pp. 394-398.

[111] S. Piramuthu, "On learning to predict Web traffic", *Decision Support Syst.*, vol. 35, pp. 213– 229, 2003.

[112] D. Xing and J. Shen," Efficient data mining for Web navigation patterns", *Inform. and Software Technology*, vol. 46, pp. 55–63, 2004.

[113] Q.Yang *et al.*, "Web-log cleaning for constructing sequential classifiers", *Appl. Artificial Intell.*, vol.17. no.5, pp. 431-441, 2003.

[114] X.Wang *et al.*,"Intelligent Web traffic mining and analysis", *J. of Network and Comput. Applicat.*, vol. 28, pp. 147–165, 2005.

[115] N. Khasawneh and C.Chan, "Web Usage Mining Using Rough Sets", in *Proc. of the Annu. Meeting of the North Amer. Fuzzy Inform. Processing Soc.*, 2005, pp. 581-585.

[116] Y. Yang and B. Padmanabhan, "GHIC: A Hierarchical Pattern-Based Clustering Algorithm for Grouping Web Transactions", *IEEE Trans. Knowl. Data Eng.*, vol. 17, no. 9, pp. 1300-1304, 2005.

[117] Z. Hong-fang *et al.*, "Mining User Preferred Knowledge from Web-Log", in *Proc. of the Int. Conf. on Computational Intell. and Security*, Guangzhou, 2006, pp.121-124.

[118] Q. Song and M. Shepperd, "Mining Web browsing patterns for E-commerce", *Comput. in Ind.*, vol. 57, pp. 622–630, 2006.

[119] H. K. Tripathy and B. K. Tripathy, "A Rough set approach for clustering the Data Using Knowledge Discovery in World Wide Web for E-Business", in *Proc. of the IEEE Int. Conf. on e- Bus. Eng.*, Hong Kong, 2007, pp. 717-722.

[120] M. Agosti and G. M. Nunzio," Web Log Mining: A Study of User Sessions", in *Proc. of the 10th DELOS Thematic Workshop on Personalized Access, Profile Manage., and Context Awareness in Digital Libraries*, Corfu, Greece, 2007, pp.1-5.

[121] L. Chaofeng and L. Yansheng, "Similarity Measurement of Web Sessions Based on Sequence Alignment", *Wuhan Univ. J. of Natural Sci.*, vol. 12, no. 5, pp. 814-818, 2007.

[122] P. Kumar *et al.*, "Rough Clustering of Sequential Data", *Data & Knowledge Eng.*, vol. 63, pp. 183-199, 2007.

[123] G. Pallis *et al.*, "Validation and interpretation of Web users' sessions clusters", *Inform. Process. and Manage.*, vol.43, pp. 1348–1367, 2007.

[124] S. Alam *et al.*, "Particle Swarm Optimization Based Clustering Of Web Usage Data", in *Proc. of the IEEE/WIC/ACM Int. Conf. on Web Intell. and Intelligent Agent Technology*, 2008, Sydney, NSW, pp.451-454.

[125] S. Park *et al.*, "Sequence-based clustering for Web usage mining: A new experimental framework and ANN-enhanced K-means algorithm", *Data & Knowledge Eng.*, vol. 65, pp. 512–543, 2008.

[126] M. E. Snyder *et al.*, "Preprocessing DNS Log Data for Effective Data Mining", in *Proc. of the IEEE Int. Conf. on Commun.*, Dresden, 2009, pp. 1366-1370.

[127] Jyoti *et al.*, "A Novel Approach for clustering Web user sessions using RST", in *Proc. of the Int. Conf. on Advances in Computing, Control, and Telecomm. Technologies*, Trivandrum, India, 2009, pp.657-659.

[128] L.Chen *et al.*, "COWES: Web user clustering based on evolutionary Web sessions", *Data & Knowledge Eng.*, vol. 68, pp. 867–885, 2009.

[129] Y. Yang, "Web user behavioral profiling for user identification", *Decision Support Syst.*, vol. 49, pp. 261–271, 2010.

[130] M.Munk *et al.*," Data Preprocessing Evaluation for Web Log Mining: Reconstruction of Activities of a Web Visitor", *Procedia Comput. Sci.*, vol.1, pp. 2273-2280, 2010.

[131] P. Zhu and M.Zhao, "Session Identification Algorithm for Web Log Mining", in *Proc. of the Int. Conf. on Manage. and Service Sci.*, Wuhan, 2010, pp.1-4.

[132] H. Xinhua and W. Qiong, "Dynamic Timeout-Based A Session Identification Algorithm", in *Proc. of the Int.Conf. on Electric Inform. and Control Eng.*, Wuhan, China, 2011, pp.346-349.

[133] K. Suresh et al., "Improved FCM algorithm for Clustering on Web Usage Mining", in *Proc. of the Int. Conf. on Comput. and Manage.*, Wuhan, China, 2011, pp.1-4.

[134] S. Vijayalakshmi et al., "Extracting Sequential Access Pattern from Pre-processed Web Logs", in *Proc. of the Int. Conf. on Process Automation, Control and Computing*, Coimbatore, India, 2011, pp.1-6.

[135] H. Hao et al., "Separating Interleaved User Sessions from Web Log", in *Proc. of the Int. Conf. on Network Computing and Inform. Security*, Guilin, 2011, pp.152-156.

[136] R. Paneerselvam, *Research Methodology*, Prentice Hall of India, 2nd ed., 2004.

[137] K. L. Wu et al., P. S. Yu & A. Ballman, "SpeedTracer: A Web usage mining and analysis tool", *IBM Syst. J.*, vol. 37, no. 1, pp. 89-105, 1998.

[138] P. Liu and W. Li, "Navigation Pattern Discovery on Website Based on the Distance Between Sequences", in *Proc. of the 2nd Int. Conf. on Artificial Intell., Manage. Sci. and Electron. Commerce*, Deng Leng, 2011, pp. 2200-2202.

[139] B. Plaza, "Monitoring Web traffic source effectiveness with Google Analytics" *Aslib Proc.: New Inform. Perspectives,* vol. 61, no. 5, pp. 474-482, 2009.

[140] C.R. Kothari, *Research Methodology Methods & Techniques*, New Age Int. Publishers, 2nd ed., 2004.

[141] K.G.C Nair et al., *A Systematic Approach to Business Statistics*, Chand Publishers, 2001.

[142] B. Mobasher et al., "Creating Adaptive Websites Through Usage-Based Clustering of URLs", in *Proc. of the Workshop on Knowledge and Data Eng. Exchange,* Chicago, IL, 1999, pp.1-7.

[143] R. Srikant and Y.Yang, "Mining Web Logs to Improve Website Organization", in *Proc. of the 10th Int. World Wide Web Conf.*, Hong Kong, 2001, pp. 430-437.

[144] C. Chen, "Discovery of User Preferred Access Patterns from Web Logs", in *Proc. of the 8th Int. Conf. on Fuzzy Syst. and Knowledge Discovery (FSKD)*, Shanghai, China, 2011, pp.419-423.

[145] W. Tong and H.Pi-Lian," Find Duration Time Maximal Frequent Traversal Sequence on Websites", in *Proc. of the IEEE Int. Conf. on Control and Automation, Guangzhou*, 2007, pp.2136-2139.

[146] C. Yang *et al.*, "Research on User Access Sequence Mining Based on the Duration Time of Web Page", in Proc. of the Int. Conf. on Web Inform. Syst. and Mining, Sanya, 2010, pp. 72-75.

[147] N.Shan *et al.*, "Using Rough Sets as Tools for Knowledge Discovery", in *Proc.of KDD-95*, 1995, pp.263- 268.

[148] M. Magnani, "Technical report on Rough Set Theory for Knowledge Discovery in Data Bases", Knowledge Discovery in Databases, 2003, pp. 1-18, Available: http://citeseerx.ist.psu.edu/viewdoc/ download? doi–10.1.1.10.9036&rep=rep1&type=pdf.

[149] A.I. Dimitras *et al.*,"Business failure prediction using rough sets", *European J. of Operational Research*, vol. 114, pp. 263-280,1999.

[150] Z. Pawlak," Rough set approach to knowledge-based decision support", *European J. of Operational Research*, vol. 99, pp. 48-57, 1997.

[151] P. Gogoi *et al.*, "Efficient Rule Set Generation using Rough Set Theory for Classification of High Dimensional Data", *Int. J. of Smart Sensors and Ad Hoc Networks*, vol.1, no. 2, 2011, pp. 13-20.

[152] S. Lee and M.Huang, "Applying AI technology and rough set theory for mining association rules to support crime management and fire-fighting resources allocation", *J. of Inform.,Technology and Soc.* vol. 2, pp. 65-78, 2002.

[153] J. Li and N. Cercone, "A Rough Set Based Model to Rank the Importance of Association Rules", *Lecture Notes in Artificial Intell.* vol. 3642, pp. 109-118, 2005.

[154] C. Liao and K. Hsu, "A Rule-Based Classification Algorithm: A Rough Set Approach", in *Proc. of the IEEE Int. Conf. on Computational Intell. and Cybern.*, Bali, 2012, pp.1-5.

[155] M. K. Sabu and G. Raju, "Rule Induction using Rough Set Theory – An Application in Agriculture", in *Proc. of the Int. Conf. on Comput., Commun. and Elect. Technology*, Tamil Nadu, 2011, pp.45-49.

[156] D. Sullivan, *Webspin*. (2003). Newslett. [online]. Available http://contentmarketingpedia.com/Marketing-Library/Search/ industry NewsSeptA1.pdf, Retrieved December 4, 2012.

[157] L. Vaughan and M. Thelwall, "Search Engine Coverage Bias: Evidence and Possible Causes", *Inform. Process. and Manage.*, vol. 40, no.4, pp. 693-707, 2004.

[158] J. Bhagwani and K. Hande, "Context Disambiguation in Web Search Results Using Clustering Algorithm", *Int. J. of Comput. Sci. and Commun*, vol. 2, no.1, pp. 119-123, 2011.

[159] F. Schwenke and M. Weideman, "The influence that JavaScript has on the visibility of a Website to search engines – a pilot study", *Informatics & Design Papers and Reports*, vol.11, no.4, pp. 1-10, 2006.

[160] M. Thelwall, "A Web Crawler Design for Data Mining", *J. of Inform. Sci.*, vol. 27, no.5, pp. 319-325, 2001.

[161] O. Brandman, "Crawler-Friendly Web Servers", *SIGMETRICS Newslett.*, vol. 28, no.2, pp.9-14, 2000.

[162] M. Drott, "Indexing aids at corporate Websites: The use of robots.txt and meta tags", *Inform. Processing and Manage.*, vol.38, no.2, pp. 209-219, 2002.

[163] L. Giles et al.,"Measuring the Web Crawler Ethics", in *Proc. of the 19th Int.WWW Conf.*, Raleigh, USA, 2010, pp. 1101-1102.

[164] W. H. Kruskal and W. A.Wallis, "Use of Ranks in one-criterion Variance analysis", *J. of the Amer. Statistical Assoc.*, vol. 47, no. 260, pp. 583-621, 1952.

[165] Y. Sun *et al.*, "A Large-Scale Study of Robots.txt", in *Proc. of the 16th Int. WWW conf.*, Banff, Canada, 2007, 1123-1124.

[166] S.Brin and L. Page, "The Anatomy of a Large Scale Hypertextual Web Search Engine", *Comput. Networks and ISDN Syst.* vol.30, pp. 107- 117, 1998.

[167] M. C. Drott, "Using Web Server Logs to Improve Site Design", in *Proc. of the 16th Annu. Int. Conf. on Comput Documentation*, 1998, pp. 43-50.

[168] S. Raghavan and H. Garcia-Molina, "Crawling the Hidden Web", *Tech. Repo.,2000-36*, Computer Science Department, Stanford University, December 2000. Available at http://dbpubs.stanford.edu/pubs/2000-36

[169] A. Heydon and M. Najork, "Mercator: A scalable, extensible Web crawler", *World Wide Web*, vol.2, no. 4, pp.219-229, 1999.

[170] F. M. Gordon and P. Pathak, "Finding information on the World Wide Web: the retrieval effectiveness of search engines", *Inform. Processing and Manage.*, vol. 35, pp. 141-80, 1999.

[171] D. Sullivan, "Major Search Engines and Directories", [online], Available: http://www.leepublicschools.net/Technology/Search-Engines_Directories.pdf, Retrieved on May 15, 2013.

[172] D. Chatterjee, "Web Mining for Pattern Discovery in E-Commerce Applications", *Master of Sci. Thesis*, Univ. of Nagpur, India, 2001.

[173] M. Thelwall, "The Responsiveness of Search Engine Indexes", *Int. J. of Scientometrics, Informetrics and Bibliometrics,* vol. 5, no. 1, pp. 1-10, 2001.

[174] F.Menczer et al., "Evaluating Topic Driven Web Crawlers", *in Proc. of the 24th annu. Int. ACM SIGIR conf. on Research and development in inform. retrieval,* New Orleans, 2001, pp. 241-249.

[175] H. Chen et al.," MetaSpider: Meta-Searching and Categorization on the Web", *J. of the Amer. Soc. for Inform. Sci. and Technology*, vol. 52, no. 13, pp. 1134–1147, 2001.

[176] M. Chau et al., "Personalized Spiders for Web Search and Analysis", in *Proc of the 1st ACM/IEEE-CS joint conf. on Digital libraries,* Virginia, 2001, pp. 79-87.

[177] M. Thelwall, "Methodologies for Crawler Based Web Surveys", *Internet Research,* vol. 12, no.2, pp.124-138, 2002.

[178] M. R. Henzinger, "Algorithmic Challenges in Web Search Engines", Internet Mathematics, vol. 1, no. 1, pp. 115-126, 2003.

[179] L. Wel and L. Royakkers, "Ethical issues in Web data mining", *Ethics and Inform. Technology*, vol. 6, pp. 129–140, 2004.

[180] D. Tanasa and B. Trousse, "Advanced Data Preprocessing for Intersites Web Usage Mining"*, Intelligent Systems*, vol. 19, no. 2, pp.59-65, 2004.

[181] O. Papapetrou and G.Samaras, "Minimizing the Network Distance in Distributed Web Crawling", in *Proc of the Int. Conf. on Cooperative Inform. Syst.*, Larnaca, 2004, pp. 581-596.

[182] A. Ntoulas et al., "What's New on the Web? The Evolution of the Web from a Search Engine Perspective", in *Proc. of the 13th Int. Conf. on World Wide Web*, New York, 2004, pp. 1-12.

[183] J. X. Yu *et al.*, "Identifying Interesting Visitors through Web Log Classification", *IEEE Intell. Syst.*, vol. 20, no. 3, pp.55-59, 2005.

[184] P. Srinivasan *et al.*, "A General Evaluation Framework for Topical Crawlers", *Inform. Retrieval*, vol.8, no.3, pp. 417-447, 2005.

[185] B. J. Jansen and A. Spink, "How Are We Searching The World Wide Web?: A Comparison Of Nine Search Engine Transaction Logs", *Inform. Processing and Manage.*, vol. 42, no. 1, pp. 248-263, 2006.

[186] F. McCown *et al.*," Lazy Preservation: Reconstructing Websites by Crawling the Crawlers", in *Proc. of the 8th annu. ACM int. workshop on Web inform. and data manage.*, Virginia, 2006, pp. 67 – 74.

[187] B. J. Jansen, "Search log analysis: What it is, what's been done, how to do it", *Library & Inform. Sci. Research*, vol. 28, pp. 407–432, 2006.

[188] J. Engler and A. Kusiak, "Web Mining for Innovation", *ABI/INFORM Global*, vol. 130, no.11, pp. 38-40, 2008.

[189] R. Nath and S. Bal, "A Novel Mobile Crawler System Based on Filtering off Non-Modified Pages for Reducing Load on the Network", *The Int. Arab J. of Inform. Technology*, vol. 8, no. 3, pp.272-279, 2011.

[190] M. P. Dikaikos *et al.*, "An Investigation of Web Crawler Behavior: Characterization and Metrics", *Comput. Commun.*, vol. 28, pp.880-897, 2005.

[191] http://www.alexa.com/help/Webmasters, retrieved on May 10, 2013.

[192] http://www.Webmasterworld.com/search_engine_spiders/4348357.htm, retrieved on May 10, 2013.

[193] http://user-agent-string.info/list-of-ua/bot-detail?bot=bingbot, retrieved on May 15, 2013.

[194] http://whatis.riskyinternet.com/what-is/Web-robot/discoveryengine-robot-6142/ , retrieved on May 10, 2013.

195 http://www.rhyolite.com/anti-spam/badbots.html, retrieved on May 10, 2013.

196 http://support.google.com/Webmasters/bin/answer.py?hl=en&answer=178852, retrieved on May 10, 2013.

197 http://support.google.com/Webmasters/bin/answer.py?hl=en&answer=182072, retrieved on May 15, 2013.

198 http://www.majestic12.co.uk/projects/dsearch/, retrieved on May 10, 2013.

199 http://www.bing.com/blogs/site_blogs/b/Webmaster/archive/2009/08/10/crawl-delay-and-the-bing-crawler-msnbot.aspx, retrieved on May 10, 2013.

200 http://help.yahoo.com/help/us/ysearch/slurp, retrieved on May 10, 2013.

201 http://blocklistpro.com/content-scrapers/ahrefsbot-seo-spybots.html, retrieved on May 10, 2013.

202 http://www.robots.txt.org/wc/robots.html, retrieved on May 10, 2013.

203 http://www.robotstxt.org/db/magpie.html, retrieved on May 10, 2013.

204 http://www.stat.cmu.edu/~hseltman/309/Book/chapter7.pdf, retrieved on May 10, 2013.

205 D. B. Duncan, "Multiple range and multiple F tests", *Biometrics II*, pp.1-42, 1955.

206 A. Tripathy and P. K. Patra, "A Web Mining Architectural Model of Distributed Crawler for Internet Searches Using PageRank Algorithm", *in Proc. of the Asia-Pacific Services Computing Conf.*, Yilan, 2008.

207 T. Linda and S. Greenberg,"Revisitation Patterns in World Wide Web Navigation", in *Proc. of the ACM SIGCHI Conf. on Human factors in Computing Syst.*,Atlanta, USA, 1997, pp. 22-27.

208 E. Adar *et al.,* "Large Scale Analysis of Web Revisitation Patterns", in *Proc. of the SIGCHI Conf. on Human Factors in Computing Syst.,* Florence, 2008, pp. 1197-1206

[209] M. R. Meiss *et al.*, "Ranking Websites with Real User Traffic", in *Proc. of the Int. Conf. on Web Search and Data Mining*, Stanford, 2008, pp. 65-76.

[210] Y. Zhang *et al.*, "Time series analysis of a Web search engine transaction log", *Inform. Process. and Manage.*, vol.45, pp. 230–245, 2009.

[211] C. Olston and S. Pandey, "Recrawl Scheduling Based on Information Longevity", in *Proc of the 17th Int. Conf. on World Wide Web*, Beijing, 2008, pp.437-446.

[212] Y.S. Kim *et al.*, "Coverage and Delay Forecast Modeling of Search Engine Services", [online] Available. http://www.academia.edu/3252414/Coverage_and_Delay_Forecast_Modeling_of_Search_Engine_Services, Retrieved on May 10, 2013

[213] S. Lawrence and C. L. Giles, "Accessibility of Information on the Web", *Nature*, vol. 400, no. 107, pp. 107-109, 1999.

[214] V. Shkapenyuk and T. Suel, "Design and Implementation of a High-Performance Distributed Web Crawler", in *Proc. of the 18th Int. Conf. on Data Eng.*, Washington, DC, USA, pp. 357-368, 2002.

[215] S. Bal and R. Nath, "Filtering the Web Pages that are not modified at Remote Site without Downloading using Mobile Crawlers", *Inform. Technology J.*, vol. 9, no. 2, pp. 376-380, 2010.

[216] J. Cho et al.," Efficient crawling through URL ordering", in *Proc of the 7th Int. World Wide Web Conf.*, Brisbane,1998.

[217] B. Pinkerton, "WebCrawler:Finding What People Want", *Ph.D Thesis, Univ. of Washington*, 2000.

[218] K.Koht-Arsa, "High Performance Cluster Based Web Spiders", *Master of Eng. Thesis, Kasetsart Univ.*, 2003.

[219] M. Koster, "Robots in the Web: threat or treat?", 1995, [online], Available: www.robotstxt.org/threat-or-treat.html, retrieved on May 15, 2013.

[220] J. Han and M. Kamber, *Data Mining Concepts and Techniques*, 3rd ed., Elsevier, 2012.

[221] M. H. Dunham, *Data Mining Introductory and advanced Topics*, Prentice Hall, 2003.

[222] S. Jaggia," Forecasting with ARMA Models", *CS-BIGS*, vol. 4, no. 1, pp. 59-65, 2010.

[223] G. Box and G. Jenkins, *Time-Series Analysis: Forecasting and Control*, 2nd ed., San Francisco, CA: Holden Day, 1984.

[224] G. Weisang and Y. Awazu, "Vagaries of the Euro: an Introduction to ARIMA Modeling", *CS-BIGS*, vol. 2, no.1, pp.45-55, 2008.

[225] W. W.S Wei, *Time Series Analysis: Univariate and Multivariate Methods*, 2nd ed., Pearson Educ., 2006.

[226] P. J. Brockwell and R. A. Davis, *Time Series: Theory and Methods*, Springer, 1991.

[227] G. P. Zhang, "Time Series Forecasting using a Hybrid ARIMA and Neural Network Model", *Neurocomputing*, vol. 50, pp. 159-175, 2003.

[228] S. Makridakis and M. Hibon," Arma Models and the Box-Jenkins Methodology", *J. of Forecasting*, vol. 16, no. 3, pp.147-163, 1984.

..........ಬಿಲ..........

List of Publications evolved out of this Thesis

a) International Journals

[229] Jeeva Jose and P. Sojan Lal, "Application of ARIMA(1,1,0) for Predicting Time Delay of Search Engine Crawlers", *Informatica Economica*, vol. 17, no. 4, 2013, pp. 26-38. DOI: 10.12948/issn14531305/ 17.4.2013.03

[230] Jeeva Jose and P. Sojan Lal, "Differences in Time Delay between Search Engine Crawlers at Web sites", *International Journal of Software and Web Sciences*, vol. 2, no. 5, 2013, pp.112-117. ISSN: 2279-0071

[231] Jeeva Jose and P. Sojan Lal, "Mining Web Logs to Identify Search Engine Behavior at Web sites", *Informatica*, vol. 37, no. 4, 2013, pp.381-386. ISSN: 1854-3871

[232] Jeeva Jose and P. Sojan Lal, "Analysis of the Temporal Behavior of Search Engine Crawlers at Web sites", *COMPUSOFT: International Journal of Advanced Computer Technology*, vol. 2, no. 6, 2013, pp.136-142. ISSN: 2320-0790

[233] Jeeva Jose and P. Sojan Lal, "A Forecasting Model for the Pages Crawled by Search Engine Crawlers at a Web Site", *International Journal of Computer Applications(IJCA)*, vol. 68, no. 13, 2013, pp.19-24. DOI: 10.5120/11639-7122

[234] Jeeva Jose and P. Sojan Lal, "An Indiscernibility Approach for Pre-processing of Web Log Files", *International Journal of Internet Computing*, vol. 1, no. 3, 2012, pp.58-61. ISSN: 2231-6965

[235] Jeeva Jose and P. Sojan Lal, "Extracting Extended Web Logs to Identify the Origin of Visits and Search Keywords", *Intelligent Informatics*,

Advances in Intelligent Systems and Computing, Springer, vol. 182, 2012, pp. 435-441. DOI: 10.1007/978-3-642-32063-7_46

b) International Conferences

[236] Jeeva Jose and P. Sojan Lal, "A Rough Set Approach to Identify Content and Navigational Pages at a Website", Proceedings of the IEEE International Multi Conference on Automation, Computing, Control, Communication and Compressed Sensing, organized by St. Joseph's College of Engineering Pala, March 22-23, 2013. ISBN: 978-1-4673-5089-1.

[237] Jeeva Jose and P. Sojan Lal, "Discovery of Similar User Sessions from the Entry Point to a Website", 10th International Conference on ICT and Knowledge Engineering, IEEE, organized by Siam University, Bangkok, Thailand, November 21-23, 2012. ISBN: 978-1-4673-2314-7.

[238] Jeeva Jose and P. Sojan Lal, "Extracting Extended Web Logs to Identify the Origin of Visits and Search Keywords", Proceedings of the International Symposium on Intelligent Informatics, organized by RMK Engineering College, Chennai, August 4-5, 2012. pp. 435-441. ISBN: 978-3-642-32062-0 [Selected for publication in Intelligent Informatics, Springer (Publication 235)].

[239] Jeeva Jose and P. Sojan Lal, "Analysis of the Sequence Length of Visitors from the Entry Point and their Repeated Visits", Proceedings of the International Conference on Data Science and Engineering, IEEE, organized by Department of Computer Science, CUSAT, Cochin, July 18-20, 2012, pp.179-183. ISBN: 978-1-4673-2146-4.

[240] Jeeva Jose and P. Sojan Lal, "An Indiscernibility Approach for Pre-processing of Web Log Files", Proceedings of the International

Conference on Electrical Engineering and Computer Science, IRNet, Trivandrum, May 12, 2012, pp.39-43. ISBN: 978-93-81693-58-2[Selected for publication in International Journal of Internet Computing (Publication 234)].

c) National Conferences

[241] Jeeva Jose and P. Sojan Lal, "Clustering of Users based on Entry Pages to Analyze the deep linked traffic at a Business Organization's Web Site", National Conference on Advanced Computing and Communication Technology, organized by Santhigiri, College of Computer Sciences, Thodupuzha, November 15-16, 2012. ISBN : 978-81-9245-812-0.

Appendix

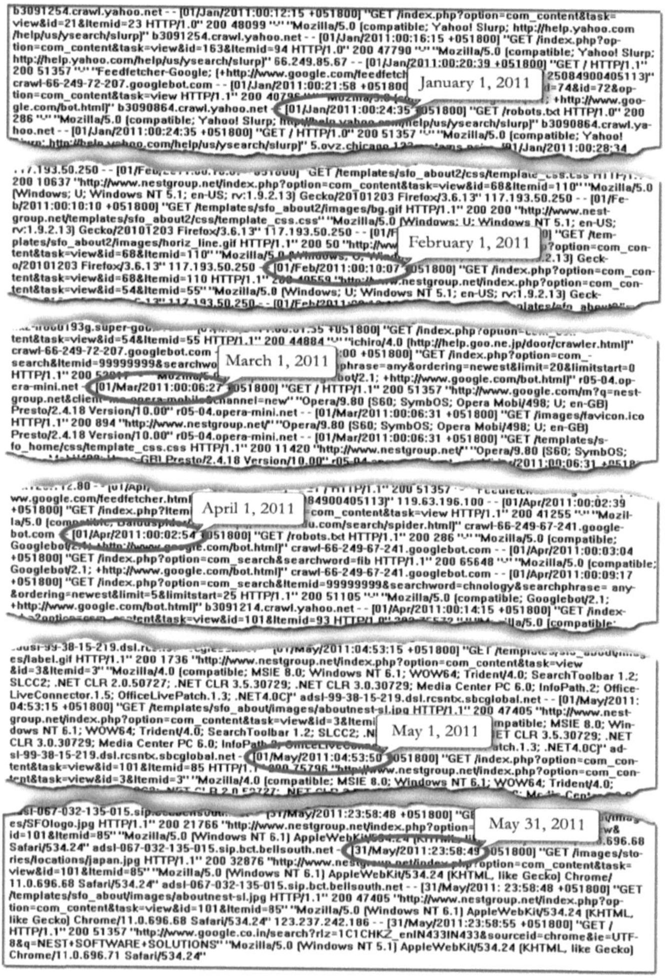

Fig. A.1 Web log of business organization NeST ranging from January 1, 2011 to May 31, 2011

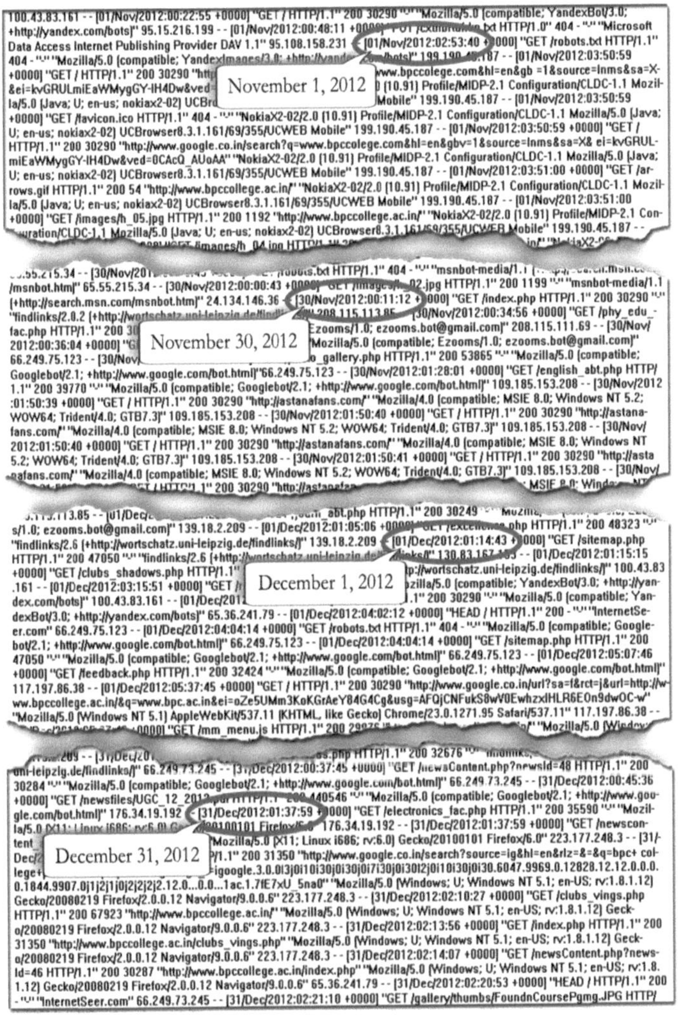

Fig. A.2 Web log of academic institution BPC College ranging from November 1, 2012 to December 31, 2012

...........ಇಲ್ಲ..........